Additional Praise For
Basic Accounting Simplified

"Finally, there is a book on the market with an easy-to-grasp formula that can help bewildered students, confused bookkeepers, and anybody with his or her own business to understand the principles of accounting. Basic Accounting Simplified provides practical insight into the world of accounting."
—**Bruce J. Temkin**, *author of The Terrible Truth About Investing*

"With its fresh approach, clear language, memory aids, and visual illustrations, *Basic Accounting Simplified* makes the basics of accounting easy to understand."
—**Peter Gulia**, *Fiduciary Guidance Counsel, Philadelphia, PA*

"They say that one picture is worth a thousand words and this book is yet further proof of that statement. The charts and diagrams are extremely well done, and make a complicated subject easy to understand."
—**Mac Brown**, *President, Doctors Financial Management Group, Orlando, FL*

"Why struggle with accounting concepts? This is the first book to explain a practical system in a readily understood manner."
—**Lester J. Mantell**, *CPA, JD, LLM, New York, NY*

"A straightforward, step-by-step process makes difficult concepts easy to understand."
—**Richard Epstein**, *CPA, New York, NY*

"It's nicely laid out, tightly written, and makes sense from start to finish."
—**Gordon Burgett**, *author of Niche Publishing, Novato, CA*

"A great overview. By simplifying complex concepts, like subsidiary ledgers and the general ledger, you will be able to more easily think through, understand, and master the more difficult issues that will be taught as your accounting education progresses."
—**Sam D. Arkind**, *Former IRS Training Instructor, Brooklyn, NY*

"… a great supplementary teaching guide. Best used before the class begins, then looked at during class, and kept as a reference later."
—**Bernard I. Rader**, *CPA, Freeport, NY*

BASIC ACCOUNTING SIMPLIFIED

Alvin L. Lesser, PA and Gary S. Lesser, JD

GSL Galactic Publishing
www.BasicAccountingSimplified.com
(317) 254–0385

Revised: July 2023

ISBN 978-0-999-32295-6

2 3 4 5 6 7 8 9 0

About the Authors

Alvin L. Lesser, PA., practiced public accounting in New York for over 35 years. He was also a licensed real estate broker and commercial property developer. After serving in the military, Alvin received his B.A. in Accounting from New York University. Before computers came into popular usage, Alvin developed a method that substantially shortened the time to complete a set of books.

Gary S. Lesser, JD, is a nationally known author, educator, and speaker. He is also the technical editor and co-author of Aspen Publishers' *Health Savings Account Answer Book, Roth IRA Answer Book, 457 Answer Book,* and *Quick Reference to IRAs*. Gary is also the principal author and technical editor of *The CPA's Guide to Retirement Plans for Small Businesses* and other publications of the American Institute of Certified Public Accountants (AICPA).

Gary graduated from New York Law School and received his B.A. in accounting from Fairleigh Dickinson University. He is admitted to the bars of the state of New York and the United States Tax Court.

Introduction

When the basics are understood, the more advanced aspects of accounting are easier to understand. By simplifying complex concepts, *Basic Accounting Simplified* helps students of accounting to think through, understand, and master the more difficult issues that will be taught as their accounting education progresses.

Basic Accounting Simplified also provides a practical approach to solving problems. Straightforward instructions will guide the student through this process and will engage the student every step of the way.

The objective of this book is to impart *an in-depth understanding of the fundamentals of accounting* to the beginning or struggling accounting student. It presents an easy-to-grasp technique that can be mastered in a short time. This book:

> ➤ Uses a unique teaching method that takes the stress out of learning the basics in order to make it easier to learn more complex accounting principles

> ➤ Explains journal entries and their relation to the trial balance

> ➤ Displays and explains the journals and ledgers and all postings

> ➤ Exhibits a full set of accounting books

> ➤ Covers the steps necessary to make financial statements

Basic Accounting Simplified is the "safety net" every accounting student should have to be successful in this field.

Overview

Chapter 1   The Method

The basics of accounting, including the trial balance, are discussed and thoroughly explained in this chapter.

- Learning the basics of accounting
- The large scope of double-entry accounting
- Journal entries and how to make them
- Examples of journal entries
- Journal entries and posting to the Trial Balance
- A completed trial balance made by journal entry

Chapter 2   Ledgers, Journals, and the Trial Balance

The various books of account are discussed and explained in this chapter. The relationship between journals and ledgers and the trial balance are analyzed and examined in this chapter. The following ledgers and journals are included:

- The General Ledger
- The Subsidiary Ledgers
- The Check Disbursement Journal
- The Cash Receipts Journal
- The Purchase Journal and Accounts Payable Ledger
- The Sales Journal and Accounts Receivable Ledger
- The Commission Ledger and Petty Cash Book

Chapter 3   Combining Journals and Ledgers

The "books of account" will be combined and provide a thorough overview of accounting. Making postings, journals, and ledgers, are explained in this chapter.

Chapter 4   Student Practice Session: Posting From Journals to Ledgers

The student will complete the posting from completed journals to ledgers. The posting from the Check Disbursement Journal, the Cash Receipts Journal, the Purchase Journal, and the Sales Journal are examined in this chapter.

Appendices

Contents

Chapter 3

Chapter 4

Appendices

Chapter 1
The Method

1. Introduction

The practice or profession of accounting is more of a science than an art. The double-entry system of accounting provides assurance errors have not been made. Business transactions are recorded in journals in a well-defined manner. The recordation into the general ledger provides a pathway to the Trial Balance and ultimately to the Balance Sheet and Profit and Loss statement.

This book employs a unique method of instruction in that it starts with the first phase of the accounting process, the journal entry, and skips to the last phase, the trial balance, completely omitting journals and ledgers. This will facilitate the understanding of journals and ledgers as they are later explained in Chapter 2. Slowly and gradually, a complete set of accounting books will be created. The steps involved in making a financial record of business transactions and in the preparation of statements concerning the Balance Sheet and income are fully discussed and explained.

2. Chapter Objective

To learn the basics of accounting up to and including the trial balance. When the basics are understood, the more advanced aspects of accounting will be more easily understood. The following figure is an important illustration. It should be kept in mind now and throughout your accounting career (see also, Figure 1-3 located below in Section 5A).

The following diagram is illustrative of one of the most basic concepts in accounting. Debits and credits can be good or bad for the business. Simply knowing whether an item is good or bad for the business and whether it is a balance sheet or profit and loss item can be used to determine whether the item is posted as a debit or credit.

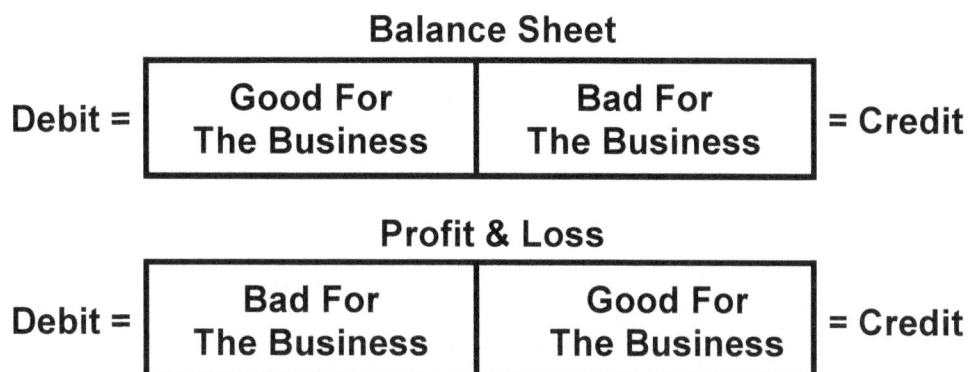

Balance Sheet

Debit =	Good For The Business	Bad For The Business	= Credit

Profit & Loss

Debit =	Bad For The Business	Good For The Business	= Credit

Figure 1-1

The illustration shows that:

- A balance sheet item that is *good* for the business is a *debit.*
- A balance sheet item that is *bad* for the business is a *credit.*
- A profit and loss item that is *good* for the business is a *credit.*
- A profit and loss item that is *bad* for the business is a *debit.*

3. The Journal Entry

A journal entry is the method used in accounting to record business transactions. The journal entry could be very simple by having just one debit and one credit. It could also have one debit and ten credits. It does not matter how many debits or credits a journal entry has, but the cardinal rule is *the total of the debits must equal the total of the credits* in every journal entry. All areas of accounting utilize journal entries. When information is recorded in any book of account it is done by journal entry, for example.

- When data is posted to the general ledger it is posted by journal entry
- When the numbers in the general ledger are netted, a journal entry is formed in the balance column
- When the netted amounts are placed on the trial balance it is a journal entry

Helpful Tip. A *debit* is always on the left side and a *credit* is always on the right side. There is an "r" in **credit** and **right**.

4. The Trial Balance

In the system of instruction ("The Method") used in Chapter 1, all journal entries will be posted directly to the trial balance. In figure 1-2, below, in the first two columns following the "Item" column is an illustration of the Trial Balance to which all the journal entries that follow later in this chapter will be posted. The adjusting entries and the financial statements are made after the trial balance has been entered in those columns.

Helpful Tip. As will be discussed later in this book, transactions are recorded using journal entries and the trial balance. At the end of each accounting period and after all the preparatory work has been done, the results are recorded in the general ledger. The net amounts contained in the general ledger are then recorded onto the trial balance.

For instructional purposes, all the journal entries in Chapter 1 will be posted directly to the trial balance. Journal entry items that affect the balance sheet are placed under the caption balance sheet items, and those that affect profit and loss are placed in that designated area on the trial balance. Since they are separated in name only, a journal entry that affects both the balance sheet and profit and loss are placed in their respective areas.

Item	Trial Balance Balance Sheet Items		Adjusting Entries		Balance Sheet	
	Debit	Credit	Debit	Credit	Debit	Credit
	Profit & Loss Items				Profit & Loss	

Figure 1-2

5. The Balance Sheet

The balance sheet maintains a permanent, but ever changing record, of the financial matters that affect a business. It shows the financial position of a business at any specific moment in time. The balance sheet is comprised of assets (shown as debits) and liabilities (shown as credits). As shown in Figure 1-3, assets are represented by the word **Good**. All the good items a business possesses, such as money in the bank, accounts receivable, and so on, are assets and are *good*. The liabilities are the opposite and are represented by the word ***Bad***. To put it simply *good* in the balance sheet minus *bad* equals the Owner's Equity which, as shown, is on the credit side, but nevertheless is shown as *good*. The reason it is shown as *good* is explained later.

Examples of some of the items carried on the balance sheet are:

- *Accounts Payable* maintains a *record* of the total amount owed to the vendors when merchandise or services are purchased on credit.

- *Accounts Receivable* maintains a *record* of the total amount owed by purchasers when merchandise or services are sold on credit.

- *Inventory* maintains a *record* of the relative value of the merchandise on hand at the beginning and at the end of the accounting period.
- *Loans Payable* maintains a *record* of who is owed money and how much is owed.
- *Equipment* maintains a record of trucks, cars, and other equipment owned by the Star Company.
- *Petty Cash* maintains a record of the cash available for reimbursement of miscellaneous expenditures made on behalf of the Star Company.
- Bank keeps a record of the amount of cash in the bank.

Balance sheet items are those items that maintain a record as long as the business is in existence. The balance sheet items that exist at the end of an older accounting period also exist on the first day of the next (new) accounting period.

A. Assets

Assets are all the items in the possession of a business that are good for the business. Having more money in the bank, larger accounts receivable, more inventory and equipment, and so on, reflect a thriving business. All assets are debits and placed in the first quadrant of Figure 1-3.

TRIAL BALANCE WITH QUADRANTS				
Debits		**Balance Sheet**	**Credits**	
GOOD	**Quadrant 1**	**BAD**	**Quadrant 2**	
Assets		**Liabilities**		
		Owner's Equity Good		
Debits		**Profit & Loss**	**Credits**	
BAD	**Quadrant 3**	**GOOD**	**Quadrant 4**	
Losses		**Profits**		

Figure 1-3

B. Liabilities

Liabilities are all the items in the possession of a business that are bad for the business. Being overdrawn at the bank, large accounts payable, too many loans and notes payable, etc., may be indications of a business in dire straits. Balance sheet items that are bad for the business are displayed as credits in the second quadrant of Figure 1-3.

6. Profit and Loss Items

Profit and loss items are the normal income and expense items associated with a business. At the end of the accounting period, the expenses are subtracted from sales and other income items and the profit or loss is determined. This profit or loss is transferred by journal entry to the owner's equity account (discussed in chapter 4). The closing entry is such that all the profit and loss items become zero at the beginning of the new accounting period. As the new accounting period progresses, the new income and expense amounts build up and, at the end of the new accounting period they are, once again, transferred to *owner's equity*. Thus, this process is repeated for each accounting period.

Examples of items that appear in the balance sheet area or in the profit and loss area on the trial balance are shown in Table 1-1, below.

Table 1-1. Balance Sheet and Profit and Loss Items

Balance Sheet Items	Profit & Loss Items
• Accounts Payable	• Advertising
• Accounts Receivable	• Auto Expense
• Bank	• Commission
• Deposits	• Electric
• Equipment	• Food and Lodging
• Furniture & Fixtures ("F&F")	• Purchases
• Equipment	• Rent
• Inventory	• Sales
• Loans Payable	• Telephone
• Owner Equity	
• Petty Cash	

Table 1-1

Note. Throughout the book there will be many references to the word "account." When this word is used, reference is being made to one of the items listed in the *chart of accounts* shown in Section 7.

7. Chart of Accounts

The *chart of accounts* serves the same function in accounting as the table of contents found at the beginning of a book. The chart, provided by the accountant, provides the bookkeeper with the means of determining the accounts included in the *general ledger* and their page numbers within the general ledger. The *chart of accounts* for the Star Company, a small manufacturing business, is shown below.

Chart of Accounts	
General Ledger	**GL #**
Balance Sheet Items*	
Accounts Payable (Control)	7
Accounts Receivable (Control)	3
Bank	1
Deposits	4
Inventory	10
Loans Payable	8
Owner's Equity	9
Equipment	5
Petty Cash	2
Reserve for Depreciation	6
Profit and Loss Items *	
Auto Expense	53
Commission	54
Food and Lodging	55
Depreciation	58
Profit & Loss	59
Purchases	52
Rent	56
Telephone	57
Sales	51

* The word "item" is used, at times, when referring to a specific item in the chart of accounts. It is primarily used when referring to the balance sheet or the profit and loss statement. For example, a balance sheet item means that it belongs in the balance sheet portion of the trial balance. Conversely, a profit and loss item means it belongs in the profit and loss portion of the trial balance.

8. The Wide Scope of Double-Entry Accounting

All of accounting is primarily a journal entry. A journal entry is, first and foremost, an example of double-entry accounting. It doesn't seem logical to be able to record one transaction using the same number two times. No other area in mathematics uses the same number twice. Why doesn't using the same number twice lead to duplications and erroneous answers? Why does double-entry accounting work?

A journal entry consists of two parts, a debit and a credit. For example, in the case of a sale, one of the journal entry parts is entered on the balance sheet and the other half is entered on the profit and loss. The fact the same number is entered two times works in accounting because the part put on the balance sheet keeps a record of what has transpired in the profit and loss portion. The point to remember is that each half of a journal entry performs a different function. There are exceptions to this rule that will be discussed later.

Example. Assume the following:

A.   A cash sale for $100 was made; the money is deposited into the bank.

B.   A $200 sale was made and the money is placed in the cash register.

C.   A $300 sale was made on credit.

	TRIAL BALANCE		
Debits	**Balance Sheet**	**Credits**	
(A) *Bank*	*100*		
(B) *Cash*	*200*		
(C) *Accounts Receivable*	*300*		
	Profit & Loss		
		(A) Sale	*100*
		(B) Sale	*200*
		(C) Sale	*300*

Figure 1-4

In the above example, the amount of sales ($100, $200, and $300) is known. But, equally important, there is a record of what was acquired as a result of the sales (bank, cash, and a receivable). As additional transactions are recorded, the principle remains the same: the items that keep a record are placed in the balance sheet and the items that describe the sales and expenses are placed in the profit and loss sections.

- Each time part of a journal entry is placed on the balance sheet a record is being kept

- Each time part of a journal entry is placed in the profit and loss, income or loss is affected

Helpful Tip. The double-entry accounting system serves as an error-detection system: if at any point the debits do not equal the corresponding credits, an error has occurred.

9. Types of Journal Entries

A. The Diagonal Journal Entry

A diagonal journal entry going from quadrant 1 to quadrant 4 is good for the business since it increases the probability of making a profit. A diagonal journal entry going from quadrant 3 to quadrant 2 is bad for the business since it increases the probability of suffering a loss, see Figure 1-5.

Diagonal journal entries are the most prevalent types of journal entry; more than 95 percent of all journal entries are *diagonal*. For example, depositing money in the bank as a result of a sale (quadrant 1 to 4) is a common occurrence. Withdrawing money from the bank for a purchase (quadrant 3 to 2) is also a common occurrence.

	Trial Balance		
Debits	**Balance Sheet**	**Credits**	
QUADRANT 1		QUADRANT 2	
GOOD		BAD	
Debit	**Profit & Loss**	**Credit**	
QUADRANT 3		QUADRANT 4	
BAD		GOOD	

Figure 1-5

For centuries the books of account have been set up recognizing the great frequency of these types of transactions. It is the very foundation of double entry accounting. When a sale is made, profit is affected, and the bank account is increased by the extent of the sale. When a purchase is made, loss is affected, and the bank account is decreased to the extent of the purchase.

Items that affect income adversely are placed in quadrant 3. Many of the same expenses that an individual has in operating a household would be in quadrant 3. Items that have a negative impact on income include cleaning, rent, purchases, auto expenses, utilities, telephone, etc. If an entry is made to quadrant 3, the other half of that entry must go to quadrant 2, which keeps a record of how quadrant 2 is adversely affected (e.g., a reduction in the bank account or an increase in accounts payable).

B. The Horizontal Journal Entry

Horizontal journal entries go from quadrant 1 to quadrant 2 or from quadrant 3 to quadrant 4. For example, purchasing equipment (quadrant 1), with funds withdrawn from the bank (quadrant 2), is an example of a horizontal journal entry.

Horizontal journal entries that go from quadrant 1(assets) to quadrant 2 (liabilities) only affect the balance sheet. Income is not affected when horizontal journal entries are placed in the balance sheet. Following are examples of horizontal type balance sheet journal entries. It should be noted the total of the assets and the liabilities remain the same after a horizontal entry is made to the balance sheet.

- When an error has been committed.

To record an overcharge to B Co. that should have been charge to A Co.	Debit	Credit
Accounts Receivable—A Co.	10	
Accounts Receivable—B Co.		10

- When equipment has been purchased.

To record purchase of an automobile.	Debit	Credit
Automobile	30,000	
Bank		30,000

- When the owner invests money in the business.

To record owner's investment.	Debit	Credit
Bank	10,000	
Owner's Equity		10,000

- When money is borrowed.

Money is borrowed from the bank.	Debit	Credit
Bank	5,000	
Loan Payable-Smith Bank		5,000

- Petty Cash fund is established.

	Debit	Credit
Establishment of a petty cash fund.		
Petty Cash Fund	30	
Bank		30

Note. There are very few journals entries that go horizontally from quadrant 3 (expense) to quadrant 4 (income). Horizontal journal entries that go from quadrant 3 to quadrant 4 are used mainly to correct errors.

C. Section Summary

➢ In general, there are two types of diagonal journal entries. On type goes from the asset side of the balance sheet to the income side of the profit and loss. The other type goes from the expense side of the profit and loss to the liability side of the balance sheet.

➢ There are two types of horizontal journal entries. One type goes from the asset side of the balance sheet to the liability side of the balance sheet. The other type goes from the expense side of the profit and loss to the income side of the profit and loss. Horizontal journal entries are primarily used to rectify an error, to make an adjustment, or to record the purchase of a capital asset (and have no affect on profit and loss).

TRIAL BALANCE					
DEBITS		**Balance Sheet**		CREDITS	
GOOD	**Quadrant 1.**		**BAD**	**Quadrant 2.**	
Assets			Liabilities		
			Owner's equity Good		
DEBITS		**Profit & Loss**		CREDITS	
BAD	**Quadrant 3.**		**GOOD**	**Quadrant 4.**	
Loss			Profit		

More than 95 percent of all journal entries are *diagonal*. They are either:
- A debit to quadrant 1 and a credit to quadrant 4
  - This is an entry that increases profit, or
- A debit to quadrant 3 and a credit to quadrant 2
  - This is an entry that decreases profit.

10. Practice Questions

Using Table 1-1 and the diagrams below, respond to the following questions. The correct response is indicated.

Balance Sheet Items	Profit & Loss Items
• Accounts Payable • Accounts Receivable • Bank • Deposits • Equipment • Furniture • Inventory • Loans Payable • Owner Equity • Petty Cash	• Advertising • Auto Expense • Commission • Electric • Food and Lodging • Purchases • Rent • Sales • Telephone

Table 1-1

Balance Sheet

Debit =	**Good For The Business**	**Bad For The Business**	= Credit

Profit & Loss

Debit =	**Bad For The Business**	**Good For The Business**	= Credit

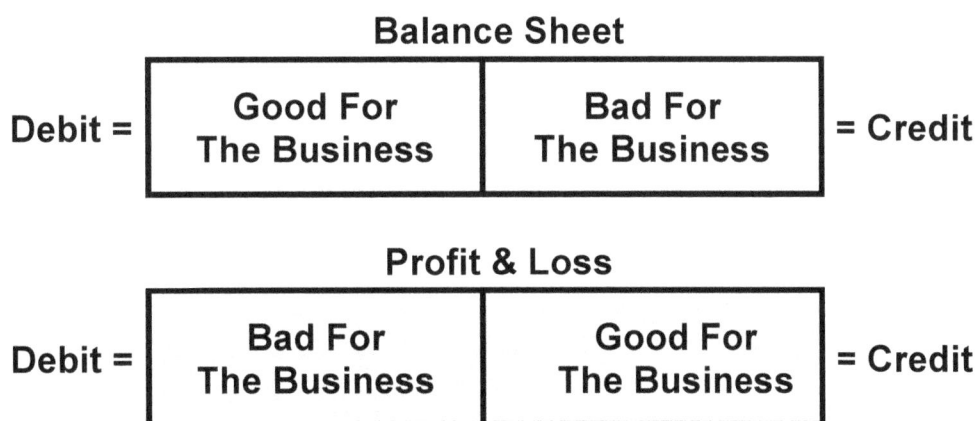

Balance Sheet Item + **Good** = Is a **Debit**	Balance Sheet Item + **Bad** = Is a **Credit**
Profit and Loss Item + **Bad** = Is a **Debit**	Profit and Loss Item + **Good** = Is a **Credit**

a) A $100 sale is made and the check is deposited in the bank. What should be your line of reasoning in regard to making the journal entry?

Reasoning:	Response:
a. What two accounts are involved in the transaction?	Sales and Bank
b. What account should be debited?	Bank. *Bank* is a *balance sheet* item. Depositing money into the bank is *good* for the business. A Balance Sheet item that is good for the business is a *debit*.
c. What account should be credited?	Sales. *Sales* is a profit and loss item and are *good* for the business. A profit and loss item that is good for the business is a *credit*.

b) A business purchases $ 200 worth of merchandise on credit. What should be your line of reasoning in regard to making the journal entry?

Reasoning:	Response:
a. What two accounts are involved in the transaction?	Purchases and Accounts Payable
b. What account should be debited?	Purchases. The account *purchases* is a *profit and loss* item. Purchases are *bad* for the business. A profit and loss item that is bad for the business is a *debit*.
c. What account should be credited?	Accounts Payable. *Accounts payable* is a *balance sheet* item. Owing money is *bad* for the business. A balance sheet item that is bad for the business is a *credit*.

c) **A business issues a $500 check to a commissioned salesman. What should be you line of reasoning in regard to making the journal entry?**

Reasoning:	Response:
a. What two accounts are involved in the transaction?	Bank and Commission
b. What account should be debited?	Commission. *Commission* is a *profit and loss* item. Paying a commission is *bad* for the business. A profit and loss item that is bad for the business is a *debit*.
c. What account should be credited?	Bank. *Bank* is a *balance sheet* item. Withdrawing money from the bank (having less cash) is *bad* for the business. A balance sheet item that is bad for the business is a *credit*.

d) **A business sells a product on credit for $300. What should be the line of reasoning in regard to making the journal entry?**

Reasoning:	Response:
a. What two accounts are involved in the transaction?	Accounts Receivable and Sales
b. What account should be debited?	Accounts receivable. *Accounts receivable* is a *balance sheet item*. Being owed money is *good*. A balance sheet item that is good for the business is a *debit*.
c. What account should be credited?	Sales. The account *sales* is a profit and loss item. A sale is *good* for the business. A profit and loss item that is good for the business is a *credit*.

11. Examples of Journal Entries and Posting to the Trial Balance

Four transactions unrelated to the Star Company are shown below. The transactions explain the reasoning involved in determining whether the transaction is posted as a debit or a credit, and whether the item affects the balance sheet or profit and loss.

Example A. A check for $1,000 is issued as payment for rent. The journal entry is as follows:

Journal Entry A	Debit	Credit
Rent	1,000	
Bank		1,000

If posted to the trial balance, the entry would appear this way.

TRIAL BALANCE			
Debits	**Balance Sheet Items**		**Credits**
		Bank (a)	1,000
		Bad	
Debits	**Profit & Loss**		**Credits**
Rent (a)	1,000		
Bad			

Reasoning

The account *Rent* is a profit and loss item (see Table 1-1). Paying rent is bad for the business. A profit and loss item that is bad for the business is a debit. Expenses are always *debits*.

The account *Bank* is a balance sheet item (see Table 1-1). Withdrawing funds from the bank is bad for the business. A balance sheet item that is bad for the business is a credit. Taking money out of the bank is always a *credit*.

Helpful Tip. A debit is always on the left side and a credit is always on the right side. There is an "r" in *credit* and r*ight*.

Example B. A $2,000 check is deposited into the checking account from a sale. The journal entry is as follows:

Journal Entry B	*Debit*	*Credit*
Bank	2,000	
Sale		2,000

If posted to on the trial balance, the entry would appear this way.

TRIAL BALANCE		
Debits	**Balance Sheet Items**	Credits
Bank (b)	$2,000	
Good		
Debits	**Profit & Loss**	Credits
	Sales (b)	$2,000
	Good	

Reasoning

     The account *Bank* is a balance sheet item (see Table 1-1). Depositing funds to the bank is good for the business. A balance sheet item that is *good* for the business is a *debit*.

     The account *Sales* is a profit and loss item. A profit and loss item that is good for the business is a credit. *Sales* are always *credits*.

Example C. A \$3,000 sale is made on credit. The journal entry is as follows:

Journal Entry C	_Debit_	_Credit_
Accounts Receivable	3,000	
Sale		3,000

TRIAL BALANCE				
Debits	**Balance Sheet Items**		**Credits**	
Accounts Receivable (c)	$3,000			
Good				
Debits	**Profit & Loss**		**Credits**	
		Sales (c)	$3,000	
		Good		

Reasoning

   Accounts Receivable is a balance sheet item (see Table 1-1). Having greater _accounts receivable_ is good for the business. A balance sheet item, good for the business, is a debit

   The account _Sales_ is a profit and loss item (see Table 1-1). _Sales_ are always good for the business. A profit and loss item that is good for the business is a credit. _Sales_ are always _credits_.

Example D. Merchandise is purchased for $1,500 on credit. The journal entry is:

Journal Entry D	*Debit*	*Credit*
Purchase	1,500	
Accounts Payable		1,500

If posted to on the trial balance, the entry would appear this way.

TRIAL BALANCE			
Debits	**Balance Sheet Items**		**Credits**
		Accounts Payable (d)	1,500
		Bad	
Debits	**Profit & Loss**		**Credits**
Purchase (d)	$1,500		
Bad			

Reasoning

The account *Purchases* is a profit and loss item. *Purchases* reduce profit and are bad for the business. Any profit any loss item that is bad for the business is a *debit*.

Accounts payable maintains a record and is a balance sheet item. To owe money is bad for the business. Any balance sheet item that is bad for the business is a *credit*.

Note. The journal entries illustrated above have been simple, having only one debit and credit. Journal entries that involve more than two items will be discussed later. At first, they will appear more complex. But when simple entries are understood, multiple entries become easy to understand.

12. Practice Journal Entries

In this section, the student will prepare the journal entries and then be shown how each entry is posted to the trial balance. The sixteen examples that follow reflect transactions of the Star Company during the current accounting period. In Chapter 4 a complete set of accounting books will be created and the entries and postings now being prepared will be used in their creation.

Use the Trial Balance (Figure 1-6) and the chart of Balance Sheet and Profit & Loss items (Table 1-2) shown below, to prepare the journal entries asked in the following questions. The "response" will display the correct journal entry and how it is posted to the trial balance. As each transaction is posted, the trial balance gets larger to accommodate the 16 journal entries.

TRIAL BALANCE				
Debits		**Balance Sheet**	**Credits**	
GOOD		BAD		
Assets		Liabilities		
		Owner's Equity Good		
Debits		**Profit & Loss**	**Credits**	
BAD		GOOD		
Losses		Profits		

Figure 1-6

Balance Sheet Items	Profit & Loss Items
• Accounts Payable	• Advertising
• Accounts Receivable	• Auto Expense
• Bank	• Commission
• Deposits	• Electric
• Equipment	• Food and Lodging
• Furniture	• Purchases
• Inventory	• Rent
• Loans Payable	• Sales
• Owner Equity	• Telephone
• Petty Cash	

Table 1-2

Journal Entry 1

Mr. Jones starts a new business, Star Company, and he borrows $5,000 from the Alpine Bank, which he deposits into the business checking account. Prepare the journal entry in the space provided below.

Journal Entry 1	Debit	Credit

Response

Mr. Jones starts a new business, Star Company, and he borrows $5,000 from the Alpine Bank, which he deposits into the business checking account. The journal entry and related entry to the trial balance are as follows:

Journal Entry 1	Debit	Credit
Bank	5,000	
Loan Payable – Alpine Bank		5,000

STAR COMPANY TRIAL BALANCE				
Debits	**Balance Sheet Items**		**Credits**	
Bank (1)	*5,000*	*Loan Payable – Alpine Bank (1)*	*5,000*	
Debits	**Profit & Loss**		**Credits**	

Reasoning

The account *bank* is a *balance sheet item* (see table at beginning of this section). A balance sheet item that is *good* for the business is entered as a debit.

Balance Sheet Item + Good = Is a Debit

The account *loan payable* is a *balance sheet* item. Having loans is *bad* for the business and is entered as a credit.

Balance Sheet Item + Bad = Is a Credit

Helpful Tip. Whether a debit or credit is good or bad depends entirely upon whether it is a balance sheet or profit and loss item.

Journal Entry 2

Star Company buys $3,500 worth of stars on credit for resale. The stars are purchased from the following sources: $1,400 from Comet, $1,200 from Asteroid, and $900 from Nebula. Prepare the journal entry in the space provided below.

Journal Entry 2	_Debit_	_Credit_

Response

Star Company buys $3,500 of stars for resale on credit. The stars are purchased from the following sources: $1,400 from Comet, $1,200 from Asteroid, and $900 from Nebula. The journal entry and related entry to the trial balance are as follows:

Journal Entry 2	_Debit_	_Credit_
Purchases	3,500	
Accounts Payable – Comet		1,400
Accounts Payable – Asteroid		1,200
Accounts Payable – Nebula		900

Note. The present journal entries are shown on the Star Company Trial Balance in *italics*; prior entries are shown in black type.

STAR COMPANY TRIAL BALANCE				
Debits		**Balance Sheet Items**	**Credits**	
Bank (1)	5,000	*Accounts Payable – Comet (2)*		*1,400*
		Accounts Payable – Asteroid (2)		*1,200*
		Accounts Payables – Nebula (2)		*900*
		Loan Payable – Alpine Bank (1)		5,000
Debits		**Profit & Loss**	**Credits**	
Purchases (2)	*3,500*			

Reasoning

Purchases are a *profit and loss item* and are *bad* for the business (see table at beginning of this section). Profit and loss items that are bad for the business are *debits*.

Profit and Loss Item *plus* Bad = Is a Debit

Accounts payable is a *balance sheet item*. Owing money is *bad* for the business. A balance sheet item that is bad for the business is a *credit.*

Journal Entry 3

Star Company issues check #101 in the amount of $60 to Seaside Telephone for phone usage. Prepare the journal entry in the space provided below.

Journal Entry 3	*Debit*	*Credit*

Response

Star Company issues check #101 in the amount of $60 to Seaside Telephone for phone usage. The journal entry and related entry to the trial balance are as follows:

Journal Entry 3	*Debit*	*Credit*
Telephone	60	
Bank #101		60

STAR COMPANY TRIAL BALANCE				
Debits		**Balance Sheet**	**Credits**	
Bank (1)	5,000	Accounts Payable – Comet (2)		1,400
		Accounts Payable – Asteroid (2)		1,200
		Accounts Payables – Nebula (2)		900
		Bank #101 (3)		***60***
		Loan Payable – Alpine Bank(1)		5,000
Debits		**Profit & Loss**	**Credits**	
Purchases (2)	3,500			
Telephone (3)	***60***			

Reasoning

The account *telephone* is a *profit and loss* item. Paying the telephone bill reduces profit and is *bad* for the business. A profit and loss item that is bad for the business is a *debit*.

The account b*ank* is a *balance sheet item*. A balance sheet item that is *bad* for the business is a *credit*.

Helpful Tip. Profit and loss items, unlike the balance sheet items, stay on the books only to the end of the accounting period, and then they eliminated. As will be shown later, any income (or loss) for the current accounting period is transferred, by journal entry, to Owner's Equity. At the end of the accounting period, a closing entry is made, which wipes the books clean of any vestiges of profit and loss items in the general ledger.

Journal Entry 4

Star Company sells $7,500 worth of stars on credit, as follows: $2,400 to Venus, $2,500 to Mars, and $2,600 Pluto. Prepare the journal entry in the space provided below.

Journal Entry 4	*Debit*	*Credit*

Response

Star Company sells $7,500 worth of stars on credit, as follows: $2,400 to Venus, $2,500 to Mars, and $2,600 Pluto. The journal entry and related entry to the trial balance are as follows:

Journal Entry 4	*Debit*	*Credit*
Accounts Receivable – Venus	2,400	
Accounts Receivable – Mars	2,500	
Accounts Receivable – Pluto	2,600	
Sales		7,500

STAR COMPANY TRIAL BALANCE			
Debits	**Balance Sheet Items**	**Credits**	
Bank (1)	5,000	Accounts Payable – Comet (2)	1,400
Accounts Receivable – Venus (4)	*2,400*	Accounts Payable – Asteroid (2)	1,200
Accounts Receivable – Mars (4)	*2,500*	Accounts Payables – Nebula (2)	900
Accounts Receivable – Pluto (4)	*2,600*	Bank #101 (3)	60
		Loan Payable – Alpine Bank (1)	5,000
Debits	**Profit & Loss**	**Credits**	
Purchases (2)	3,500	*Sales (4)*	*7,500*
Telephone (3)	60		

Reasoning

Accounts receivable is a *balance sheet* item. Being owed money is *good* for the business. A balance sheet item that is good for the business is a *debit* on the balance sheet.

The account *sales* affect profit and loss. Sales are always *good* for the business. A profit and loss item that is good for the business is a *credit*.

Profit and Loss Item + Good = Is a Credit

Journal Entry 5

Star Company issues check #102 for $200 in order to set up a petty cash fund to be used to repay employees for money expended by employees on behalf of the company. Prepare the journal entry in the space provided below.

Journal Entry 5	*Debit*	*Credit*

Response

Star Company issues check #102 for $200 in order to set up a petty-cash fund to be used to repay employees for cash expended by employees on behalf of the company. The journal entry and related entry to the trial balance are as follows:

Journal Entry 5	*Debit*	*Credit*
Petty Cash	200	
Bank (check #102)		200

STAR COMPANY TRIAL BALANCE				
Debits		**Balance Sheet Items**	**Credits**	
Bank (1)	5,000	Accounts Payable – Comet (2)		1,400
Accounts Receivable – Venus (4)	2,400	Accounts Payable – Asteroid (2)		1,200
Accounts Receivable – Mars (4)	2,500	Accounts Payables – Nebula (2)		900
Accounts Receivable – Pluto (4)	2,600	Bank #101 (3)		60
Petty Cash (5)	*200*	*Bank #102 (5)*		*200*
		Loan Payable – Alpine Bank (1)		5,000
Debits		**Profit & Loss**	**Credits**	
Purchases (2)	3,500	Sales (4)		7,500
Telephone (3)	60			

Reasoning

The account petty *cash* is a *balance sheet* item (see Table 1-1). Having more petty cash is *good* for the business. A balance sheet item that is good for the business is a *debit.*

The account *bank* is a *balance sheet* item. Having less money in the bank is *bad* for the business. A balance sheet item that is bad for the business is a *credit.*

Journal Entry 6

Star Company issues check #103 in the amount of $1,100 to Jackson Furniture for the purchase of furniture and fixtures. Prepare the journal entry in the space provided below.

Journal Entry 6	*Debit*	*Credit*

Response

Star Company issues check #103 in the amount of $1,100 to Jackson Furniture for the purchase of furniture and fixtures. The journal entry and related entry to the trial balance are as follows:

Journal Entry 6	*Debit*	*Credit*
Equipment – Furniture & Fixtures	1,100	
Bank #103		1,100

STAR COMPANY TRIAL BALANCE				
Debits	**Balance Sheet Items**		**Credits**	
Bank (1)	5,000	Accounts Payable – Comet (2)		1,400
Accounts Receivable – Venus (4)	2,400	Accounts Payable – Asteroid (2)		1,200
Accounts Receivable – Mars (4)	2,500	Accounts Payables – Nebula (2)		900
Accounts Receivable – Pluto (4)	2,600	Bank #101 (3)		60
Petty Cash (5)	200	Bank #102 (5)		200
Equipment – F & F (6)	*1,100*	*Bank #103 (6)*		*1,100*
		Loan Payable – Alpine Bank (1)		5,000
Debits	**Profit & Loss**		**Credits**	
Purchases (2)	3,500	Sales (4)		7,500
	60			

Reasoning

The account Equipment–Furniture and Fixtures is a *balance sheet* item (see Table 1-1). Having furniture and fixtures ("F&F") is *good* for the business. Balance sheet items that are good for the business are *debits*.

The account *bank* is a *balance sheet* item. Withdrawing money out of the bank is *bad* for the business. Balance sheet items that are bad for the business are *credits*.

Note. The account *equipment–furniture and fixtures* from a theoretical point of view should be an expense. However, except for small expenditures, the government requires that the cost of the furniture and fixtures be written off (depreciated) over the assets' useful life. When furniture and fixtures or other equipment is to be written off over their estimated useful life (generally determined by the Department of the Treasury), the cost of the equipment is recorded on the balance sheet. At the end of each accounting period Profit and Loss is debited by the depreciation incurred and the Balance Sheet is credited for a like amount. The account depreciation and reserve for depreciation remain on the Balance Sheet. The depreciated amount is treated as an expense in the current accounting period.

Journal Entry 7

Star Company gives check #104 for $1,500 to Edgar Motors to pay for a truck to be used in the business. Prepare the journal entry in the space provided below.

Journal Entry 7	*Debit*	*Credit*

Response

Star Company gives check #104 for $1,500 to Edgar Motors to pay for a truck to be used in the business. The journal entry and related entry to the trial balance are as follows:

Journal Entry 7	*Debit*	*Credit*
Equipment	1,500	
Bank (check #104)		1,500

STAR COMPANY TRIAL BALANCE				
Debits		**Balance Sheet Items**	**Credits**	
Bank (1)	5,000	Accounts Payable – Comet (2)		1,400
Accounts Receivable – Venus (4)	2,400	Accounts Payable – Asteroid (2)		1,200
Accounts Receivable – Mars (4)	2,500	Accounts Payables – Nebula (2)		900
Accounts Receivable – Pluto (4)	2,600	Bank #101 (3)		60
Petty Cash (5)	200	Bank #102 (5)		200
Equipment – Furniture & Fixtures (6)	1,100	Bank #103 (6)		1,100
Equipment – Truck (7)	*1,500*	*Bank #104 (7)*		*1,500*
		Loan Payable – Alpine Bank (1)		5,000
Debits		**Profit & Loss**	**Credits**	
Purchases (2)	3,500	Sales (4)		7,500
Telephone (3)	60			

Reasoning

Equipment is *balance sheet* item and having equipment is *good* for the business. Balance sheet items that are good for the business are *debits*. See journal entry 6.

The account *bank* is a balance sheet item (see Table 1-1). Withdrawing money out of the bank is *bad* for the business. A balance sheet item that is bad for the business is a *credit.*

Note. The accounting treatment of the account *equipment* is the same as the treatment of the account *equipment–furniture and fixtures* (see Note following journal entry 6).

Journal Entry 8

Mr. Smith, an employee of Star Company, submits invoices for cash he has expended. He expended the following amounts: $10 for telephone usage; $20 for auto expense; and $160 for food and lodging. Prepare the journal entry in the space provided below.

Journal Entry 8	*Debit*	*Credit*

Response

Mr. Smith, an employee of Star Company, submits invoices for cash he has expended. He expended the following amounts: $10 for telephone usage; $20 for auto expense; and $160 for food and lodging. Mr. Smith is given $190 from petty cash. The journal entry and related entry to the trial balance are as follows:

Journal Entry 8	*Debit*	*Credit*
Telephone	10	
Auto expense	20	
Food and lodging	160	
Petty Cash		190

STAR COMPANY TRIAL BALANCE			
Debits	**Balance Sheet Items**	**Credits**	
Bank (1)	5,000	Accounts Payable – Comet (2)	1,400
Accounts Receivable – Venus (4)	2,400	Accounts Payable – Asteroid (2)	1,200
Accounts Receivable – Mars (4)	2,500	Accounts Payables – Nebula (2)	900
Accounts Receivable – Pluto (4)	2,600	Bank #101 (3)	60
Petty Cash (5)	200	Bank #102 (5)	200
Equipment – F & F (6)	1,100	Bank #103 (6)	1,100
Equipment – Truck (7)	1,500	Bank #104 (7)	1,500
		Petty Cash (8)	*190*
Debits	**Profit & Loss**	**Credits**	
Purchases (2)	3,500	Sales (4)	7,500
Telephone (3)	60		
Telephone (8)	*10*		
Auto expense (8)	*20*		
Food & lodging (8)	*160*		

Reasoning

The accounts *telephone*, *auto expense*, and *food & lodging* are all items of expense and affect *profit and loss*. Having expenses are *bad* for the business, and are debits.

The account *petty cash* is a *balance sheet item*. Having less petty cash is *bad* for the business and is entered as a *credit*.

Journal Entry 9

Star Company issues check # 105 in the amount of $500 to repay a portion of the $5,000 loan due to Alpine Bank. Prepare the journal entry in the space provided below.

Journal Entry 9	*Debit*	*Credit*

Response

Star Company issues check # 105 in the amount of $500 to repay a portion of the $5,000 loan due to Alpine Bank. The journal entry and related entry to the trial balance are as follows:

Journal Entry 9	*Debit*	*Credit*
Loan payable - Alpine Bank	500	
Bank		500

STAR COMPANY TRIAL BALANCE				
Debits	**Balance Sheet Items**			**Credits**
Bank (1)	5,000	Accounts Payable – Comet (2)		1,400
Accounts Receivable – Venus (4)	2,400	Accounts Payable – Asteroid (2)		1,200
Accounts Receivable – Mars (4)	2,500	Accounts Payables – Nebula (2)		900
Accounts Receivable – Pluto (4)	2,600	Bank #101 (3)		60
Petty Cash (5)	200	Bank #102 (5)		200
Equipment – F & F (6)	1,100	Bank #103 (6)		1,100
Equipment – Truck (7)	1,500	Bank #104 (7)		1,500
Loan payable (9) - Alpine bank	**500**	**Bank #105 (9)**		**500**
		Petty Cash (8)		190
Debits	**Profit & Loss**			**Credits**
Purchases (2)	3,500	Sales (4)		7,500
Telephone (3)	60			
Telephone (8)	10			
Auto expense (8)	20			
Food & lodging (8)	160			

Reasoning

Loan payable is a balance sheet item. Reducing the amount of a loan is *good* for the business. A balance sheet items that is good for a business is a *debit.*

The account *bank* is a balance sheet item. Withdrawing money out of the bank is *bad* for the business. A balance sheet item that is bad for the business is a *credit.*

Journal Entry 10

Mr. Jones withdraws $4,000 from his personal checking account and deposits the money into Star Company's checking account to be used in the business. Prepare the journal entry in the space provided below.

Journal Entry 10	*Debit*	*Credit*

Response

Mr. Jones withdraws $4,000 from his personal checking account and deposits the money into Star's checking account to be used in the business. The journal entry and related entry to the trial balance are as follows:

Journal Entry 10	*Debit*	*Credit*
Bank	4,000	
Owner's Equity		4,000

STAR COMPANY TRIAL BALANCE				
Debits		**Balance Sheet Items**	**Credits**	
Bank (1)	5,000	Accounts Payable – Comet (2)		1,400
Accounts Receivable – Venus (4)	2,400	Accounts Payable – Asteroid (2)		1,200
Accounts Receivable – Mars (4)	2,500	Accounts Payables – Nebula (2)		900
Accounts Receivable – Pluto (4)	2,600	Bank #101 (3)		60
Petty Cash (5)	200	Bank #102 (5)		200
Equipment – F & F (6)	1,100	Bank #103 (6)		1,100
Equipment – Truck (7)	1,500	Bank #104 (7)		1,500
Loan payable (9)	500	Bank #105 (9)		500
Bank (10)	*4,000*	Loan Payable – Alpine Bank (1)		5,000
		Petty Cash (8)		190
		Owner's Equity (10)		*4,000*
Debits		**Profit & Loss**	**Credits**	
Purchases (2)	3,500	Sales (4)		7,500
Telephone (3)	60			

Telephone (8)	10		
Auto expense (8)	20		
Food & lodging (8)	160		

Reasoning

The account *bank* is a balance sheet item. Depositing money into the bank is *good* for the business. A balance sheet item that is good for the business is posted as a *debit*. The owner's equity account is a balancing account and is the only account treated differently than all the others. When a business is successful it will have more assets than liabilities.

Owner's Equity = Assets minus Liabilities

Assume the only asset of a business is $10,000 in the bank and that the business has $1,000 in accounts payable. To whom does the differential in capital belong? How does accounting show the differential? Of course the differential belongs to the owner of the business. The balance sheet reflecting this difference is shown below.

	Assets	*Liabilities*
Cash in bank	$10,000	
Accounts payable		$1,000
Owner's equity		$9,000

As can be seen above, the assets ($10,000) minus the liabilities ($1,000) is equal to $9,000, the *owner's equity*. This also explains why *owner's equity* is shown in the liability section of the balance sheet.

Note. *Owner's Equity* is a balance sheet item. Accountants often refer to an *owner's equity* by other names, including:

- Personal
- Capital
- Equity
- Proprietorship

Regardless of what name is used, owner's equity represents the value of the owner's investments in the business plus profits, minus losses and minus withdrawals made by the owner.

Journal Entry 11

Star Company gives check #106 to Fern Rentals in the amount of $1,500 for the payment of the current month's rent ($500), and a deposit of $1,000 for the last two months of a five-year lease. Prepare the journal entry in the space provided below.

Journal Entry 11	*Debit*	*Credit*

Response

Star Company gives check #106 to Fern Rentals in the amount of $1,500 for the payment of the current month's rent of $500, and includes a deposit of $1,000 for the last two months of a five-year lease. The journal entry and related entry to the trial balance are as follows:

Journal Entry 11	*Debit*	*Credit*
Rent	500	
Deposit-Rent	1,000	
Bank #106		1,500

STAR COMPANY TRIAL BALANCE			
Debits		**Balance Sheet Items Credits**	
Bank (1)	5,000	Accounts Payable – Comet (2)	1,400
Accounts Receivable – Venus (4)	2,400	Accounts Payable – Asteroid (2)	1,200
Accounts Receivable – Mars (4)	2,500	Accounts Payables – Nebula (2)	900
Accounts Receivable – Pluto (4)	2,600	Bank #101 (3)	60
Petty Cash (5)	200	Bank #102 (5)	200
Equipment – F & F (6)	1,100	Bank #103 (6)	1,100
Equipment – Truck (7)	1,500	Bank #104 (7)	1,500
Loan payable (9)	500	Bank #105 (9)	500
Bank (10)	4,000	***Bank #106 (11)***	***1,500***
Deposit – Rent (11)	***1,000***	Loan Payable – Alpine Bank (1)	5,000
		Petty Cash (8)	190
		Owner's Equity (10)	4,000

	Debits	Profit & Loss	Credits	
Purchases (2)	3,500	Sales (4)		7,500
Telephone (3)	60			
Telephone (8)	10			
Auto expense (8)	20			
Food & lodging (8)	160			
Rent (11)	*500*			

Reasoning

The account *rent*, an expense, is a *profit and loss* item. Paying rent is *bad* for the business. A profit and loss item that is bad for the business is a debit

The amount deposited ($1,000) is a *balance sheet* item. It keeps a record of funds disbursed which are expected to be repaid. Since the deposit is expected to be repaid in some form it is recorded as *good* on the balance sheet.

The account *bank* is a *balance sheet* item. Withdrawing money is *bad* for the business. A balance sheet item that is bad for the business is a *credit.*

Journal Entry 12

Star Company issues checks (#107, #108, and #109) for commission as follows:

John Roberts - $450
Robert Brown - $600
Stanley Steel - $500

Prepare the journal entry in the space provided below.

Journal Entry 12   *Debit*   *Credit*

_____

_____

_____

_____

_____

_____

Response

Star Company issues checks (#107, #108, and #109) for commission as follows:

John Roberts - $450
Robert Brown - $600
Stanley Steel - $500

The journal entry and related entry to the trial balance are as follows:

Journal Entry 12	Debit	Credit
Commission – John Roberts	450	
Commission –Robert Brown	600	
Commission – Stanley Steel	500	
106 Bank		450
107 Bank		600
108 Bank		500

STAR COMPANY TRIAL BALANCE			
Debits	**Balance Sheet Items**		**Credits**
Bank (1)	5,000	Accounts Payable – Comet (2)	1,400
Accounts Receivable – Venus (4)	2,400	Accounts Payable – Asteroid (2)	1,200
Accounts Receivable – Mars (4)	2,500	Accounts Payables – Nebula (2)	900
Accounts Receivable – Pluto (4)	2,600	Bank #101 (3)	60
Petty Cash (5)	200	Bank #102 (5)	200
Equipment – F & F (6)	1,100	Bank #103 (6)	1,100
Equipment – Truck (7)	1,500	Bank #104 (7)	1,500
Loan payable (9)	500	Bank #105 (9)	500
Bank (10)	4,000	Bank #106 (11)	1,500
Deposit – Rent (11)	1,000	*Bank #107 (12)*	*450*
		Bank #108 (12)	*600*
		Bank #109 (12)	*500*
		Loan Payable – Alpine Bank (1)	5,000
		Petty Cash (8)	190
		Owner's Equity (10)	4,000
Debits	**Profit & Loss**		**Credits**
Purchases (2)	3,500	Sales (4)	7,500
Telephone (3)	60		
Telephone (8)	10		
Auto expense (8)	20		
Food & lodging (8)	160		
Rent (11)	500		
Commission – John Roberts (12)	*450*		
Commission – Robert (12)	*600*		
Commission – Stanley Steel (12)	*500*		

Reasoning

The account *commission* is a *profit and loss* item. Paying commissions reduces profit and is *bad* for the business. A profit and loss item that is bad for the business is a *debit.*

The account b*ank* is a *balance sheet* item. Withdrawing money from the bank is *bad* for the business. A balance sheet item that is bad for the business is posted as a *credit* on the balance sheet.

Journal Entry 13

Mr. Jones requests funds for his own personal use. Star Company issues check #110 for $800 to Mr. Jones. Prepare the journal entry in the space provided below.

Journal Entry 13	*Debit*	*Credit*

Response

Mr. Jones requests funds for his own personal use. Star Company issues check #110 for $800 to Mr. Jones. The journal entry and related entry to the trial balance are as follows:

Journal Entry 13	*Debit*	*Credit*
Owner's Equity	800	
Bank #110		800

STAR COMPANY TRIAL BALANCE			
Debits		**Balance Sheet Items** **Credits**	
Bank (1)	5,000	Accounts Payable – Comet (2)	1,400
Accounts Receivable – Venus (4)	2,400	Accounts Payable – Asteroid (2)	1,200
Accounts Receivable – Mars (4)	2,500	Accounts Payables – Nebula (2)	900
Accounts Receivable – Pluto (4)	2,600	Bank #101 (3)	60
Petty Cash (5)	200	Bank #102 (5)	200
Equipment – F & F (6)	1,100	Bank #103 (6)	1,100
Equipment – Truck (7)	1,500	Bank #104 (7)	1,500
Loan payable (9)	500	Bank #105 (9)	500
Bank (10)	4,000	Bank #106 (11)	1,500

Deposit – Rent (11)	1,000	Bank #107 (12)	450
		Bank #108 (12)	600
		Bank #109 (12)	500
		Bank #110 (13)	***800***
		Loan Payable –Alpine Bank (1)	5,000
		Petty Cash (8)	190
Owner's Equity (13)	***800***	Owner's Equity (10)	4,000

Debits		Profit & Loss Credits	
Purchases (2)	3,500	Sales (4)	7,500
Telephone (3)	60		
Telephone (8)	10		
Auto expense (8)	20		
Food & lodging (8)	160		
Rent (11)	500		
Commission – John Roberts (12)	450		
Commission – Robert Brown (12)	600		
Commission – Stanley Steel (12)	500		

Reasoning

The account owner's equity is a balance sheet item. However, the payment to Mr. Jones for personal use will reduce his ownership interest and is posted as a *debit*. This is more fully discussed in Journal Entry 10.

The account b*ank* is a balance sheet item. Withdrawing money from the bank is *bad* for the business. A balance sheet item that is bad for the business is posted as a credit on the balance sheet.

Journal Entry 14

Star Company issues check #111 for $1,400 to Comet to pay off its debt, thereby reducing accounts payable. Prepare the journal entry in the space provided below.

Journal Entry 14	*Debit*	*Credit*

Response

Star Company issues check #111 for $1,400 to Comet to pay off its debt, thereby reducing accounts payable. The journal entry and related entry to the trial balance are as follows:

Journal Entry 14	*Debit*	*Credit*
Accounts Payable-Comet	1,400	
Bank #111		1,400

STAR COMPANY TRIAL BALANCE			
Debits	**Balance Sheet Items**	**Credits**	
Bank (1)	5,000	Accounts Payable – Comet (2)	1,400
Accounts Receivable – Venus (4)	2,400	Accounts Payable – Asteroid (2)	1,200
Accounts Receivable – Mars (4)	2,500	Accounts Payables – Nebula (2)	900
Accounts Receivable – Pluto (4)	2,600	Bank #101 (3)	60
Petty Cash (5)	200	Bank #102 (5)	200
Equipment – F & F (6)	1,100	Bank #103 (6)	1,100
Equipment – Truck (7)	1,500	Bank #104 (7)	1,500
Loan payable (9)	500	Bank #105 (9)	500
Bank (10)	4,000	Bank #106 (11)	1,500
Deposit – Rent (11)	1,000	Bank #107 (12)	450
Accounts Payable-Comet (14)	*1,400*	Bank #108 (12)	600
		Bank #109 (12)	500
		Bank #110 (13)	800
		Bank #111 (14)	*1,400*
		Loan Payable – Alpine Bank (1)	5,000

		Petty Cash (8)	190
Owner's Equity (13)	800	Owner's Equity (10)	4,000
Debits	**Profit &**	**Loss** **Credits**	
Purchases (2)	3,500	Sales (4)	7,500
Telephone (3)	60		
Telephone (8)	10		
Auto expense (8)	20		
Food & lodging (8)	160		
Rent (11)	500		
Commission – John Roberts (12)	450		
Commission – Robert Brown (12)	600		
Commission – Stanley Steel (12)	500		

Reasoning

Accounts payable keeps a *record* of how much money is owed and is a *balance sheet* item. Reducing debt is *good*. A balance sheet item that is good for the business is a *debit*

The account bank is a *balance sheet* item. Withdrawing money from the bank is *bad* for the business. A balance sheet item that is bad for the business is posted as a credit on the balance sheet.

Journal Entry 15

Star Company deposits a check for $1,500 from Mars reducing *accounts receivable.* Prepare the journal entry in the space provided below.

Journal Entry 15	Debit	Credit

Response

Star Company deposits a check for $1,500 from Mars reducing *accounts receivable.* The journal entry and related entry to the trial balance are as follows:

Journal Entry 15	Debit	Credit
Bank	1,500	
Accounts receivable – Mars (see Journal Entry 4)		1,500

STAR COMPANY TRIAL BALANCE			
Debits	**Balance Sheet Items**		**Credits**
Bank (1)	5,000	Accounts Payable – Comet (2)	1,400
Accounts Receivable – Venus (4)	2,400	Accounts Payable – Asteroid (2)	1,200
Accounts Receivable – Mars (4)	2,500	Accounts Payables – Nebula (2)	900
Petty Cash (5)	200	Bank #102 (5)	200
Equipment – F & F (6)	1,100	Bank #103 (6)	1,100
Equipment – Truck (7)	1,500	Bank #104 (7)	1,500
Loan payable (9)	500	Bank #105 (9)	500
Bank (10)	4,000	Bank #106 (11)	1,500
Deposit – Rent (11)	1,000	Bank #107 (12)	450
Accounts Payable-Comet (14)	1,400	Bank #108 (12)	600
Bank (15)	*1,500*	Bank #109 (12)	500
		Bank #110 (13)	800
		Bank #111 (14)	1,400
		Loan Payable – Alpine Bank (1)	5,000
		Petty Cash (8)	190
		Accounts Receivable – Mars (15)	*1,500*
Owner's Equity (14)	800	Owner's Equity (10)	4,000
Debits	**Profit & Loss**		**Credits**
Purchases (2)	3,500	Sales (4)	7,500
Telephone (3)	60		
Telephone (8)	10		
Food & lodging (8)	160		
Rent (11)	500		
Commission – John Roberts (12)	450		
Commission – Robert Brown (12)	600		
Commission – Stanley Steel (12)	500		

Reasoning

The account *bank* is a *balance sheet* item. Depositing money into the bank is *good.* A balance sheet item that is good for the business is a debit. *Accounts receivable* is a *balance sheet* item. Reducing the amount of money owed to Star Company is *bad.* A balance sheet item that is bad for the business is a credit.

Journal Entry 16

The bookkeeper from Pluto phones and informs Star Company's bookkeeper that there was a $100 overcharge on their last invoice (see Journal Entry 4). It was ascertained that Pluto had been overcharged and an adjustment is to be made. Prepare the journal entry in the space provided below.

Journal Entry 16	*Debit*	*Credit*

Response

The bookkeeper from Pluto phones and informs Star Company's bookkeeper that there was a $100 overcharge on their last invoice (see Journal Entry 4). It was ascertained that Pluto had been overcharged and an adjustment is to be made. The journal entry and related entry to the trial balance are as follows:

Journal Entry 16	*Debit*	*Credit*
Sales	100	
Accounts receivable – Pluto Co.		100

	STAR COMPANY TRIAL BALANCE EOM		
Debits	**Balance Sheet Items**	**Credits**	
Bank (1)	5,000	Accounts Payable – Comet (2)	1,400
Accounts Receivable – Venus (4)	2,400	Accounts Payable – Asteroid (2)	1,200
Accounts Receivable – Mars (4)	2,500	Accounts Payables – Nebula (2)	900
Petty Cash (5)	200	Bank #102 (5)	200
Equipment – F & F (6)	1,100	Bank #103 (6)	1,100
Equipment – Truck (7)	1,500	Bank #104 (7)	1,500
Loan payable (9)	500	Bank #105 (9)	500
Bank (10)	4,000	Bank #106 (11)	1,500
Deposit – Rent (11)	1,000	Bank #107 (12)	450
Accounts Payable-Comet (14)	1,400	Bank #108 (12)	600
Bank (15)	1,500	Bank #109 (12)	500
		Bank #110 (13)	800
		Bank # 111 (14)	1,400
		Loan Payable – Alpine Bank (1)	5,000
		Petty Cash (8)	190
		Accounts Receivable-Mars (15)	1,500
		Accounts Receivable-Pluto (16)	*100*
Owner's Equity (14)	800	Owner's Equity (10)	4,000
Debits	**Profit & Loss**	**Credits**	
Purchases (2)	3,500	Sales (4)	7,500
Telephone (3)	60		
Telephone (8)	10		
Auto expense (8)	20		
Food & lodging (8)	160		
Rent (11)	500		
Commission-John Roberts (12)	450		
Commission-Robert Brown (12)	600		
Commission-Stanley Steel (12)	500		
Sales (16)	*100*		
TOTAL TRIAL BALANCE	**30,400**		**30,400**

Pluto was overcharged by $100. Journal Entry 16 rectifies the error by reducing the amount of the sale ($100) and reducing the amount owed by Pluto ($100).

Note. Journal entry 16 was the final entry to be posted to the Trial Balance. After that posting, the balance sheet and profit and loss items were added. The totals of the trial balance ($30,400) are displayed on the bottom line. When the totals do not equal an error has been made. If an error has occurred the error or errors must be ascertained and corrected before proceeding.

The least time consuming way of correcting an error in the Trial Balance is to work backwards, as follows:

1. Check the addition in the trial balance
2. Verify the balances in the general ledger have been properly posted to the Trial Balance
3. Verify the netting out process of the general ledger has resulted in a correct balance
4. Check the posting from the ledgers to the general ledger
5. Verify the postings from the journals to the ledgers are correct

13. Calculating Profits or Loss

Adjusting entries must be made before it can be determined the amount of profit or loss the business has incurred during the accounting period. In the following explanation of how to determine profit and loss, adjusting entries will not be taken into consideration because, at this time, they are unimportant. Adjusting entries will be fully explained in Chapter 4.

Note. The Star Company Trial Balance X (shown below) is the same trial balance as in Transaction 16 above, except that the profit and loss items and the balance sheet items have been separately added.

Star Company Trial Balance X (Profit Not Shown)
EOM

Debits	**BALANCE SHEET ITEMS**	Credits
Bank (1)	5,000	Accounts Payable – Comet (2)	1,400
Accounts Receivable – Venus (4)	2,400	Accounts Payable – Asteroid (2)	1,200
Accounts Receivable – Mars (4)	2,500	Accounts Payables – Nebula (2)	900
Petty Cash (5)	200	Bank #102 (5)	200
Equipment – F & F (6)	1,100	Bank #103 (6)	1,100
Equipment – Truck (7)	1,500	Bank #104 (7)	1,500
Loan payable (9)	500	Bank #105 (9)	500
Bank (10)	4,000	Bank #106 (11)	1,500
Deposit – Rent (11)	1,000	Bank #107 (12)	450
Accounts Payable-Comet (14)	1,400	Bank #108 (12)	600
Bank (15)	1,500	Bank #109 (12)	500
		Bank #110 (13)	800
		Bank # 111 (14)	1,400
		Loan Payable – Alpine Bank (1)	5,000
		Petty Cash (8)	190
		Accounts Receivable – Mars (15)	1,500
		Accounts Receivable – Pluto (16)	100
Owner's Equity (14)	800	Owner's Equity (10)	4,000
TOTAL BALANCE SHEET ITEMS	**24,500**		**22,900**

Debits	**PROFIT & LOSS ITEMS**	Credits
Purchases (2)	3,500	Sales (4)	7,500
Telephone (3)	60		
Telephone (8)	10		
Auto expense (8)	20		
Food & lodging (8)	160		
Rent (11)	500		
Commission-John Roberts (12)	450		
Commission-Robert Brown (12)	600		
Commission-Stanley Steel (12)	500		
Sales (16)	100		
Profit	**TBD***		
TOTAL PROFIT AND LOSS ITEMS	**5,900**		**7,500**

* To be determined.

When the credits in the profit and loss are greater than the debits it indicates a profit has been made. The amount of the difference indicates the amount of profit and can be computed as follows:

Total amount of credits in the Profit and Loss	$7,500
Total amount of debits in the Profit and Loss	-5,900
Profit	$1,600

The double entry system of accounting is such that when the business has made a profit, the amount of profit causes an increase in assets or a reduction in liabilities or a combination of the two.

Total amount of debits in the Balance Sheet	$24,500
Total amount of credits in the Balance Sheet	-22,900
Increase in net worth	$1,600

A summary of the above calculations are shown below.

Calculation of Profit (or Loss)

	Debits	Credits	Difference
Total Balance Sheet	24,500	22,900	(1,600)
Total Profit and Loss	5,900	7,500	1,600
Total Trial Balance	30,400	30,400	0

The chart, above, indicates a $1,600 profit has been made. The accountant then makes the following adjusting entry.

	Debit	Credit
Profit	1,600	
Owner's equity		1,600

The profit of $1,600 is shown in the Star Company Trial Balance Y, shown below.

Star Company Trial Balance Y			
EOM			
Debits	**BALANCE SHEET ITEMS**	Credits	
Bank (1)	5,000	Accounts Payable – Comet (2)	1,400
Accounts Receivable – Venus (4)	2,400	Accounts Payable – Asteroid (2)	1,200
Accounts Receivable – Mars (4)	2,500	Accounts Payables – Nebula (2)	900
Accounts Receivable – Pluto (4)	2,600	Bank #101 (3)	60
Petty Cash (5)	200	Bank #102 (5)	200
Equipment – F & F (6)	1,100	Bank #103 (6)	1,100
Equipment – Truck (7)	1,500	Bank #104 (7)	1,500
Loan payable (9)	500	Bank #105 (9)	500
Bank (10)	4,000	Bank #106 (11)	1,500
Deposit – Rent (11)	1,000	Bank #107 (12)	450
Accounts Payable-Comet (14)	1,400	Bank #108 (12)	600
Bank (15)	1,500	Bank #109 (12)	500
		Bank #110 (13)	800
		Bank # 111 (14)	1,400
		Loan Payable – Alpine Bank (1)	5,000
		Petty Cash (8)	190
		Accounts Receivable – Mars (15)	1,500
		Accounts Receivable – Pluto (16)	100
Owner's Equity (14)	800	Owner's Equity (10) + $1,600	5,600
TOTAL BALANCE SHEET ITEMS	**24,500**		**24,500**
Debits	**PROFIT & LOSS ITEMS**	Credits	
Purchases (2)	3,500	Sales (4)	7,500
Telephone (3)	60		
Telephone (8)	10		
Auto expense (8)	20		
Food & lodging (8)	160		
Rent (11)	500		
Commission-John Roberts (12)	450		
Commission-Robert Brown (12)	600		
Commission-Stanley Steel (12)	500		
Sales (16)	100		
Profit	**1,600**		
TOTAL PROFIT AND LOSS ITEMS	**7,500**		**7,500**

14. Journal Entries versus Books of Account

The information in Chapter 1 was recorded by journal entries. It was hoped the student would learn journal entries, the balance sheet, the profit and loss and the trial balance. Starting in Chapter 2 the stress will be on all the books of account.

Had the transactions that appear in Trial Balance X (see above) been recorded using standard accounting books, the resultant trial balance would be exactly the same as it appears in trial balance Z shown below.

The recording of business transactions by journal entries is unheard of in the accounting world. By looking at trial balance X and trial balance Z it can be seen how cumbersome recording by journal entry is. This is why transactions are recorded by using the accounting books as shown in Trail Balance Z.

Note the difference; when recorded by journal entry there are forty six transactions (see trial balance Y), but only fifteen when recorded using books of account (see trial balance Z, and Chapter 4).

Star Company Trial Balance Z EOM	BALANCE SHEET	
Account Name	Debit	Credit
Bank	1,890	
Petty Cash	10	
Deposit-Rent	1,000	
Accounts Receivable	5,900	
Equipment	2,600	
Accounts Payable		2,100
Loan Payable, Alpine Bank		4,500
Owner's Equity before adjusting entries		4,800*
BALANCE SHEET TOTAL	*11,400*	*11,400*
Account Name	PROFIT & LOSS	
Sales		7,400
Purchases	3,500	
Auto expense	20	
Food and Lodging	160	
Telephone	70	
Rent	500	
Commission	1,550	
Profit (no adjusting entries)	*1,600*	
PROFIT AND LOSS TOTAL	**18,800**	**18,800**

* Reconciliation of Owner's Equity

Net worth as per Trial Balance X	$ 4,000
Drawings as per Trial Balance X	− 800
Net	3,200
Profit transferred to Owner's Equity Trial Balance Y	+ 1,600
Owner's Equity as per Trial Balance Z	$ 4,800

Chapter 2
Ledgers, Journals, and the Trial Balance

1. Introduction

Examining the relationship between journals and ledgers and the trial balance is the focus of this chapter. Each journal and ledger will be shown, discussed, examined and explained. The prior chapter stressed journal entries and how they affect the Trial Balance. A business can make a trial balance by using only journal entries. However, using journal entries to make a trial balance is impractical and would quickly become cluttered and repetitious, as seen in Chapter 1.

The journals and ledgers explained in this chapter are as follows:

- General Ledger
- Subsidiary Ledgers
- Check Disbursement Journal
- Cash Receipts Journal
- Purchase Journal and Accounts Payable Ledger
- Sales Journal and Accounts Receivable Ledger
- Commission Ledger and the Petty Cash Book

From time to time, a business requires detailed information about its dealings with individual customers and creditors. Imagine a business with hundreds (or even thousands) of purchases made on credit with the transactions all recorded on pages in the *general ledger*. It would be difficult to determine the balance owed by any single customer at a specific time because of the multitude of pages in the *general ledger*. To address this need, a subsidiary ledger is used wherein each creditor and each customer are able to have their own page that can be filed alphabetically or numerically. In this manner, the *general ledger* is not encumbered with numerous pages.

A. The General Ledger

The *general ledger* is the *last* step in the *bookkeeping* phase of the accounting process prior to preparation of the trial balance. All data recorded in the accounting books ultimately end up as debits or credits in the *general ledger*. Except for the adjusting and closing entries, the *trial balance* is the final stage in the accounting process. If the Trial Balance is the goal, the General Ledger is the entryway.

The following chart is a summary showing the flow of data starting from the journals, through the General Ledger and onto the Trial Balance. The Balance Sheet and Profit and Loss statement are prepared from the Trial Balance (see Chapter 4).

Journals

- ▶ Purchase
- ▶ Sales
- ▶ Check Disbursement
- ▶ Cash Receipts

Intermediate Items

Column totals and item amounts in "general" column only

Subsidiary Ledgers

- ▶ Accounts Payable
- ▶ Accounts Receivable
- ▶ Commission

General Ledger

Trial Balance

Adjusting Entries

Balance Sheet

Profit and Loss

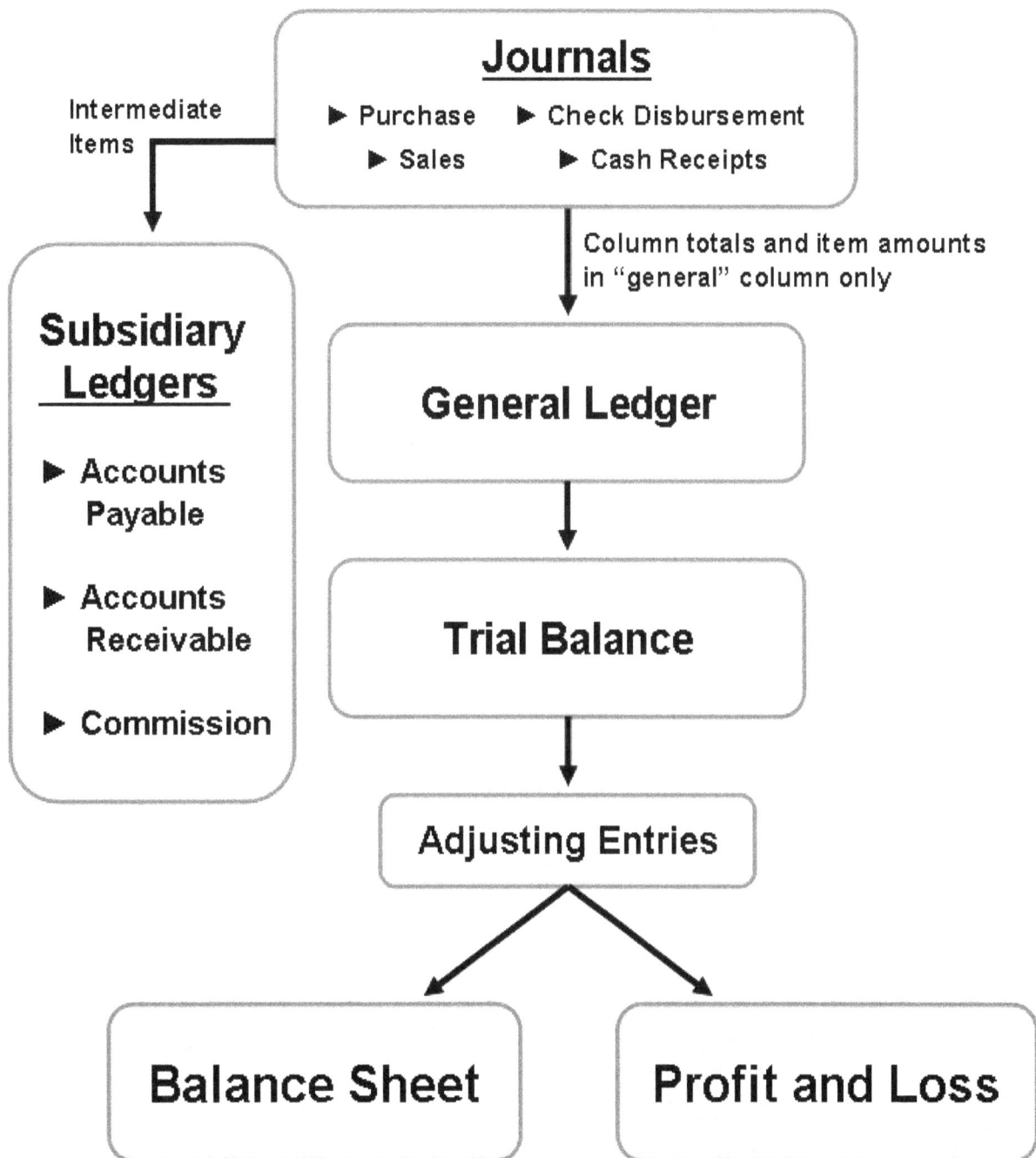

The pages in the general ledger are an accumulation of postings from all the books of account. The net amount of each page in the general ledger is placed in the Balance column of that ledger (see Figure 2-1, *Sample General Ledger Page)*. One of the main reasons for the general ledger is the netting process. Netting occurs when all the different postings on each page of the general ledger are combined and the net number is placed in the 'balance column' of the general ledger as a debit or credit.

Figure 2-1. Sample General Ledger Page

BANK		GENERAL LEDGER				GL 1
					Balance	
Date	Item	Post	Debit	Credit	Debit	Credit
EOM		CD 1		8,610		
EOM		CR 1	10,500		1,890	

The account *bank* is the first page in General Ledger and is referred to as "GL 1." The general ledger page numbers are obtained from Star Company's Chart of Accounts (discussed in subsection B, below). The net amount, $1,890 ($10,500 minus $8,600), is entered in the balance column. It is this net amount ($1,890) that is posted to the trial balance. As a result, when the totals of all the debits and credits in the trial balance are not equal, it is proof at least one error has been made in one, or more, of the postings. See Section 8 in this chapter—*Finding Errors*. The "Bank" page of the general ledger (GL 1) provides specific information, such as:

- The source of the $8,610 posting was CD 1, the Check Disbursement Journal, page 1. This means that $8,610 was expended by check during the accounting period. The total of the column "Bank" in the check disbursement journal shows the expenditure (see Section 4 in this chapter, Figure 2-9, *Completed Check Disbursement Journal*).

- The source of the $10,500 posting was CR 1, the Cash Receipts Journal, page 1. This means $10,500 was received by Star during this accounting period. The total of the column "Bank" in the *cash receipts journal* shows this receipt (see Section 9 in this chapter, Figure 2-10, *Completed Cash Receipts Journal).*

- The balance of $1,890 ($10,500 - $8,600) is recorded in the balance column of GL 1. As previously mentioned, the net amount ($1,890) will be posted to the Trial Balance when it is prepared. During this accounting period, the cash balance in the bank increased by $1,860, which is shown in the balance column of the general ledger.

Most businesses make a trial balance at the end of each month for the purpose of verifying whether an error has been made in the posting to the ledgers or to the trial balance. When a financial statement is required, the accountant uses the trial balance as a starting point, makes the adjusting entries, and creates the balance sheet and profit & loss statements. At the end of the year, the accountant generally prepares financial statements and income tax returns. It should be noted that financial statements can be prepared periodically.

There are nineteen pages in the Star Company general ledger. More pages can be added when necessary. Additional pages may need to be added, for example, when additional accounts are added and/or pages become full. Each page in the general ledger has a name corresponding to one of the names listed on the chart of accounts (see Figure 2-3, *Chart of Accounts Used in General Ledger* below).

Netting out is one of the primary reasons for having a *general ledger.* There may be many numbers in the general ledger, but only the net number in the "Balance" column is recorded onto the trial balance.

Helpful Tip. The task of the general ledger is complete when the amounts in the balance column are recorded onto the trial balance. The balance sheet and profit and loss statement are prepared from the trial balance (see Chapter 4).

B. Chart of Accounts

The bookkeeper refers to the chart of accounts to post to the general ledger. Each column in the books has a heading that contains one of the names listed on the chart of accounts, see Figure 2-3. Before posting, the bookkeeper matches the column heading with the names on the chart of accounts. For example, as shown in the chart of accounts for the Star Company, the *general ledger* page for "bank" is GL 1.

Figure 2-3. Chart of Accounts Used in General Ledger

General Ledger Chart of Accounts	GL #
Balance Sheet Items	
Accounts Payable (Control)	7
Accounts Receivable (Control)	3
Bank	1
Deposits	4
Inventory	10
Loans Payable	8
Owner's Equity	9
Equipment	5
Petty Cash	2
Reserve for Depreciation	6
Profit and Loss Items	
Auto Expense	53
Commission	54
Food and Lodging	55
Depreciation	58
Profit & Loss	59
Purchases	52
Rent	56
Telephone	57
Sales	51

2. Subsidiary Ledgers

Understanding subsidiary ledgers and the part they play in accounting is extremely important. *It is a concept that must be understood!* Subsidiary ledgers exist so that the number of pages in the general ledger can be kept to a manageable number. Depending upon the size of the business, keeping records of accounts receivable, accounts payable, and commission could require thousands of pages that would have to be added to the general ledger (explained below). The use of subsidiary ledgers makes the bookkeeping work more efficient and less costly.

Helpful Tip. Subsidiary ledgers are made from the item amounts *within* a column using the single-entry system of accounting. Subsidiary ledgers are only referred to by management and ignored by the accountant. It is the bookkeeper's function to make sure the subsidiary ledgers are in agreement with their respective pages in the general ledger.

Note. From time to time, a random sample from the Star Company's books and records is displayed and used as an illustration.

There are three *subsidiary ledgers*, each of which keeps track of one aspect of accounting (see figure 2-4, *Postings from Journals to Subsidiary Ledgers and to General Ledger*, below):

1. The *accounts receivable ledger* is made by posting the intermediate items in the accounts receivable column of the Sales Journal to the accounts receivable ledger. As payments are received, the intermediate items in the accounts receivable column in the Cash Receipts Journal are posted to the accounts receivable ledger, which keeps a record of each business that owes the Star Company money.

   ➤ The *accounts receivable ledger* is made from a column in the Sales Journal and from a column in the Cash Receipts Journal.

2. The *accounts payable ledger* keeps track of the businesses to which Star Company owes money. As purchases are made, the amount of money owed by the Star Company is recorded in the accounts payable ledger. Payments made by the Star Company are recorded in the same ledger.

   ➤ The *accounts payable ledger* is made by posting the intermediate items in the accounts payable column of the Purchase Journal to the accounts payable ledger. As payments are made by Star Company, the intermediate items in the accounts payable column in the Check Disbursement Journal are posted to the accounts payable ledger.

3. The *commission ledger* keeps track of commission payments.

> ➤ The *commission ledger* is made using the numbers in the commission column of the Check Disbursement Journal. Each recipient of commission has their own page in the commission ledger.

Three pages in the general ledger are called "control accounts" because each one of the three pages *controls* a subsidiary ledger, which could contain 100 or more pages. The three General Ledger pages and the subsidiary ledger it *controls* are shown below (but see discussion in Section 2(A), *Types of Subsidiary Ledgers*, regarding the Commission Ledger):

Control page in the general ledger	***Subsidiary ledger it controls***
Accounts Payable page GL 7	Accounts Payable Ledger (AP)
Accounts Receivable page GL 3	Accounts Receivable Ledger (AR)
Commission page GL 54	Commission Ledger (CL)

A subsidiary ledger is a group of similar accounts whose combined balances equal the balance in a specific General Ledger account. The general ledger account that summarizes its subsidiary ledger's account balances is called a "control account." For example, the accounts receivable *subsidiary* ledger includes a separate page for each customer who makes credit purchases. The combined balance of every page in this *subsidiary* ledger equals the balance of *accounts receivable* account in the General Ledger.

Helpful Tip. Column *totals* are posted to the General Ledger only.

Note. A business can have only one general ledger, but will have at least two and possibly more subsidiary ledgers. Because management wanted to know who earned commission and how much, Star Company made a *commission* ledger. It was a matter of choice.

Figure 2-4 shows how accounting information flows from the four journals to the three subsidiary ledgers described above and to the General Ledger. Intermediate item amounts (the dollar amounts shown between the column heading and the column total; see next section) are posted to one of three subsidiary ledgers. However, the column totals *and* the item amounts in the "General" column are posted only to the General Ledger. It should be noted that the total of the *general* column is not posted (but is used for cross-footing).

Figure 2-4.   Postings from Journals to Subsidiary Ledgers and to General Ledger

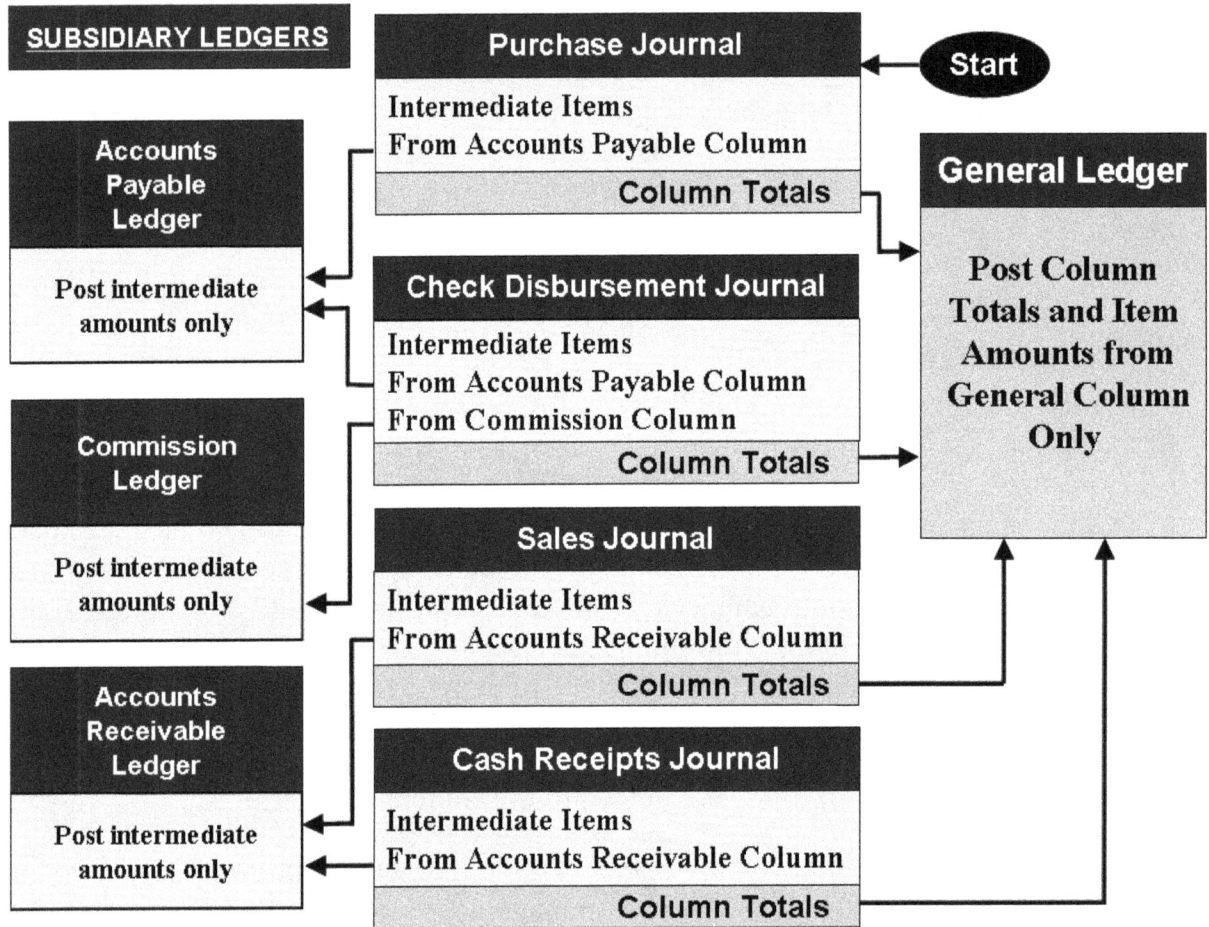

Helpful Tip. All posting to subsidiary ledgers are made using the single-entry system of accounting. This is permissible because subsidiary ledger accounts are *not* part of and are independent of the general ledger (see Section 2(E), *Journal Flow Chart,* in this chapter). The subsidiary ledgers are made for the perusal of management and other interested parties and play no part in the accounting process. Thus, details are posted to the subsidiary ledgers, but the total of the details is posted to the general ledger. As a result, the general ledger holds all the data and is all that matters in the accounting process.

A. Types of Subsidiary Ledgers

A subsidiary ledger is a group of similar accounts whose combined balances equal the balance in a specific general ledger account. The general ledger account that summarizes its subsidiary ledger's account balances is called a control account. The Accounts Payable and the Accounts Receivable Ledgers are the standard subsidiary ledgers used by most business that are on the accrual basis of accounting. Their pages in the general ledger are not only influenced by credit sales and purchases, but also by checks received as a result of sales and checks paid as a result of purchases.

Star company asked the accountant to make a subsidiary ledger so that management could see how much *commission* each recipient received without the necessity of going through the commission *column* of the check disbursement journal. As shown in Figure 2-4 above, amounts posted to the Commission Ledger come from only one source, the Check Disbursement Journal. Although the Commission Ledger is a subsidiary ledger (established at managements request), it is not really being "controlled" by the General Ledger. The accounts receivable and the accounts payable ledgers are ever changing because the balance each of those ledgers are predicated on the amounts of checks paid *and* the amounts of checks received. For those ledgers, the balance in the general ledger must equal the combined balance of the subsidiary ledger (which it controls). By contrast, the Commission Ledger of Star Company only shows a running total of all commissions paid; something management requested. The balance in the Commission ledger always increases; it never decreases *during* the accounting period. It is merely a ledger account used by management and not the accountant.

Management can, at any time, request the bookkeeper to go through the commission column in the check disbursement ledger and submit a report as to how much was paid to each commission earner. The same cannot be done with account receivable columns and accounts payable columns. For example, it cannot be determined who is owed money from Star Company by merely looking at the accounts payable column. Conversely, it cannot be determined who owes money to Star Company by merely looking that the accounts receivable column. But, nevertheless, when the accounts receivable, accounts payable, and commission columns are posted, they are all posted the same way—by the utilization of intermediate items. At the request of management many accounts in the Chart of Accounts can be converted to subsidiary ledgers.

Helpful Tip. Posting a debit or credit to a subsidiary ledger account (which is made using the single-entry system of accounting) and also to a general ledger control account does not violate the rule that total debit and credit entries must balance because subsidiary ledger accounts are not part of the "book of account;" they are supplemental accounts that provide the detail to support the balance in a control account.

B. Intermediate Items

The Star Company's purchase journal is shown as Figure 2-5, *Display of the Purchase Journal*, and is used as an illustration to explain intermediate items.

Intermediate items refer to the dollar amounts shown between the column heading and the column total (in this case, $1,400, $1,200, and $900) in the column headed *accounts payable* in the Purchase Journal (see Figure 2-5, *Display of the Purchase Journal*). Intermediate items are *always* posted to subsidiary ledgers. Although the column total ($3,500) is posted to the general ledger (GL 7), it is important to remember that intermediate items are always posted to a subsidiary ledger.

Note. Intermediate items are only located within journal columns headed *accounts payable*, *accounts receivable*, and *commission*. Intermediate items are never posted unless a subsidiary ledger is involved. Only the *accounts payable*, *accounts receivable*, and *commission* columns are posted to subsidiary ledgers.

Note. The amounts shown in the accounts payable and purchase columns (see Figure 2-5) were entered when the purchases were made. The totals of both these columns are posted to their designated pages in the general ledger (GL 7 and GL 52). The intermediate items (shown in italic type) are posted to the accounts payable ledger. A discussion of the specific posting of the intermediate items to the three pages in the accounts payable ledger are more fully explained in Section 3 of this chapter (see, "Item D̲").

Figure 2-5. Display of the Purchase Journal

PURCHASE JOURNAL							PJ 1	
Date	Account Credited	Post	**Accounts Payable** Credit	**Purchases** Debit		General	Amount Debit	
EOM	Comet Co.	AP C	*1,400*	1,400				
EOM	Asteroid Co.	AP A	*1,200*	1200				
EOM	Nebula Co.	AP N	*900*	900				
	Total		3,500	3,500				
			GL7	**GL 52**				

Caution. Amounts entered in the "Purchase" column are not intermediate items because intermediate items are only located in journal columns headed *accounts payable*, *accounts receivable*, and *commission*.

If only the intermediate items, rather than the total, were posted to the general ledger, then the general ledger would be too large and cumbersome, particularly when there were large numbers of creditors or debtors. The problem is solved by using subsidiary ledgers in place of posting to the general ledger.

The accounts receivable ledger and accounts payable ledger, both subsidiary ledgers, are almost universal in their utilization. Businesses that operate on the accrual basis of accounting use subsidiary ledgers (see Chapter 4 for explanation of accrual basis). The Star Company's use of the commission ledger, a subsidiary ledger, is a matter of choice. The vast majority of businesses do not use that ledger.

Helpful Tip. Consider the following when posting to subsidiary ledgers:

1. When posting to the *accounts payable* ledger use symbol **AP** *plus* the first letter of the creditor's last name. For example, "AP C" stands for the accounts payable subsidiary ledger page C, and represents the page in the subsidiary ledger for Comet Company (see Figure 2-5, *Display of the Purchase Journal,* "Post" column).

2. When posting to the *accounts receivable* ledger use symbol **AR** *plus* the first letter of the debtor's last name.

3. When posting to the *commission* ledger use symbol **CL** *plus* the first letter of the agent's last name.

C. Location of Columns

Columns headed *accounts payable*, *accounts receivable*, and *commission* are only located in certain journals. Those journals and the subsidiary ledger account are shown below.

Column Headings	Location of Column		Subsidiary Ledger to Which Posted
Accounts Payable	Purchase Journal and the Check Disbursement Journal	→	Accounts Payable Ledger (GL 7)
Accounts Receivable	Sales Journal and the Cash Receipts Journal	→	Accounts Receivable Ledger (GL 3)
Commission	Check Disbursement Journal	→	Commission Ledger (GL 54)

None of the other journal columns (*bank, telephone, rent, petty cash, owner's equity,* and *general*) contain intermediate items that go to subsidiary ledgers. It should be noted that items entered in the *general* column are individually posted to the *general* ledger and the general *column total* is not posted at any time.

D. Accounting's Limitation

Accounting's limitation is that an accountant is unable to post the total of accounts payable *and* the names and the amount owed each creditor with one posting. There are only two options, an accountant can either--

Method 1: Post only the total amount of accounts payable, in this case $3,500, to the *general ledger,* or

Method 2: Post the intermediate items, in this case $1,400, $1,200 and $900 (which total $3,500) to the *general ledger.*

Assume only the total ($3,500) in the accounts payable column of the purchase journal is posted to the general ledger (Method 1). In this case, the names, and so on, of the creditors would be unknown because that information is provided by the posting of intermediate items. On the other hand, if only the intermediate items, and not the total, were posted to the general ledger (Method 2), then the general ledger would be too large and cumbersome, particularly when there were a large number of creditors and debtors.

The problem is solved by using subsidiary ledgers. The *columnar total* is posted to the general ledger. The *intermediate items* are posted to the accounts payable ledger, a subsidiary ledger. By solving the problem in this manner, both the total amount of sales and the names and other information of each debtor can be recorded. These events are summarized in the following diagram.

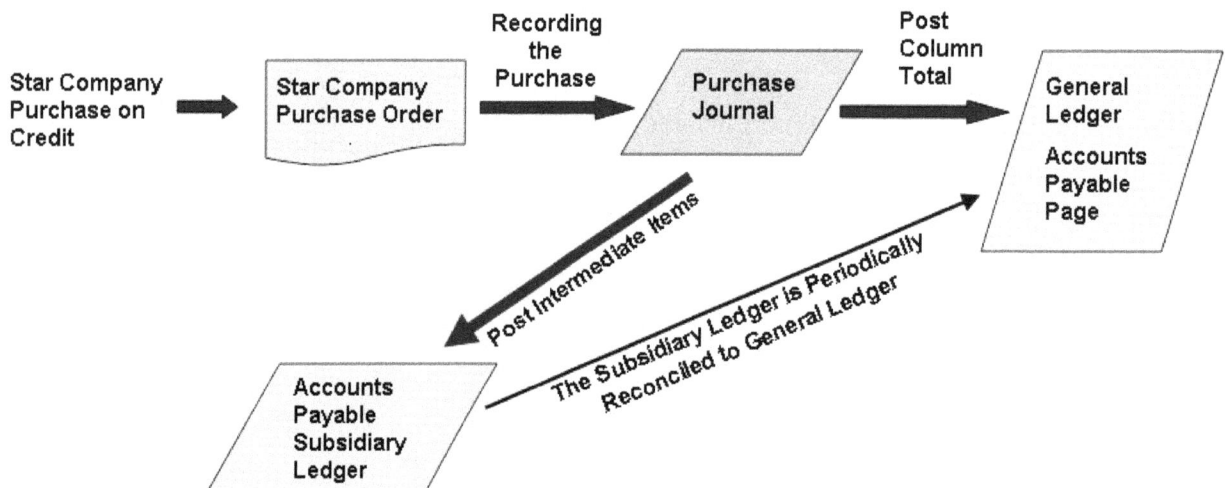

Recording the total amount of purchases to the general ledger is important because the totals in the General Ledger are used when the accountant prepares the Trial Balance. Subsidiary ledgers are relatively unimportant because they merely provide the names and the amount owed to each creditor, the total of which has already been posted to the general ledger.

Helpful Tip. "Why must intermediate items be posted to subsidiary ledgers, since the total of the intermediate items are posted to the general ledger? The purpose of subsidiary ledgers is to inform management as to the details of business transactions and to minimize the size of the general ledger. For example, if only the total of the accounts payable column in the check disbursement is posted to the general ledger, how would management know who is owed the money? If payments were made to 1,000 or more vendors how would management know who was paid and the amount paid?

Since Star Company has only 19 accounts in its general ledger, adding 1,000 more pages would make the general ledger unwieldy. It is far better to place accounts receivable in one ledger, accounts payable in a different ledger, and to place commissions in a third ledger. The separation of ledgers makes the bookkeeping work more efficient and less costly.

Example. Assume the following:

1. Star Company has 1,000 different businesses to which it owes money due to purchases it made. (An accounts payable of 1,000 different businesses.)

2. If the names, and so on, of all the creditors are put on different pages in the general ledger. There would now be 1,019 pages in the general ledger.

3. The bookkeeper and the accountant decide 1,019 pages are too many pages in the general ledger, making it too difficult to work with.

4. The accountant takes the 1,000 pages of accounts payable out of the general ledger and puts the pages in a different book called the *accounts payable ledger*.

5. The 1,000 pages in the new accounts payable ledger are totaled.

6. The total in the new accounts payable ledger is placed on one page in the general ledger.

7. From now on, the total of the accounts payable column is posted to the general ledger and the intermediate items are posted individually to the accounts payable ledger.

The result is that Star now has a *general ledger* of nineteen pages and an *accounts payable* ledger of one thousand pages. The general ledger is now a lot easier for the accountant to work with, and management has the tools it needs to operate the business.

E. Journal Flow Chart

The following chart shows the flow of data starting with the journals, through the General Ledger and onto the Trial Balance, from which the Balance Sheet and Profit and Loss statement are prepared (see Chapter 4). The posting of intermediate items in the four journals to subsidiary ledgers to prevent the over loading of the general ledger, and to supply interested parties with the details regarding sales and purchases, are also shown.

F. Observations

➢ Subsidiary ledgers exist so the number of pages in the general ledger can be kept to a manageable number.

➢ The accounts payable page (GL 7) of the general ledger controls the accounts payable ledger. The total of each must be equal to the total in the other.

➢ The accounts payable ledger is subsidiary to the accounts payable page of the general ledger (GL 7).

➢ All column totals in all of the journals ultimately end up as debits or credits in the balance column of the general ledger.

3. The Purchase Journal

The purchase journal records the items that are purchased on credit. Each purchase made on credit is recorded in the accounts payable column of the purchase journal. The three intermediate items highlighted in italic type indicate the names of the creditors. The intermediate items are posted to the accounts payable ledger, which has a separate page for each creditor containing the details pertaining to the purchases such as the address of the vender, the terms, etc. The total of the purchases ($3,500) is posted to the general ledger GL 52. The posting of the Purchase Journal are shown in Appendix C—*Purchase Journal Flow Chart* and in Appendix F—*Purchase Journal Chart*.

Figure 2-6. Display of the Purchase Journal

PURCHASE JOURNAL							PJ 1
Date	Account Credited	Post	Accounts Payable *Credit*	Purchases *Debit*	General		Amount *Debit*
EOM	Comet Co.	AP C	*C* *1,400*	1,400			
EOM	Asteroid Co.	AP A	*C* *1,200*	1200			
EOM	Nebula Co.	AP N	*C* 900	900			
	Total		*3,500*	*3,500*			
			GL7	GL 52			
			A	*B*			

Note. Items with underlined capital letters are explained below.

Helpful Tip. Intermediate items are always of the same denomination as that of the column total. If the column total in the journal is a debit, the intermediate items are debits. On the other hand, if the column total in the journal is a credit, the intermediate items are credits. The numbers in the "accounts payable" column can be extended (like purchases) in order to show the different types of items purchased. For example, the extended columns could be headed, "supplies," "sub contractor," or "lodging." The total of each of the extended items is posted to the general ledger. In this case the only extension was to purchases, the total of which is posted to the purchases page of the general ledger (GL 52).

The posting from the purchase journal to the general ledger and to the subsidiary ledgers are as follows:

Item A. From the accounts payable column of the purchase journal the total ($3,500, a credit) is posted to the *accounts payable* page of the general ledger (GL 7) as a credit, see Figure 2-7. Note the indicated source of the posting, PJ 1.

Figure 2-7. Posting of $3,500 to Accounts Payable in the General Ledger

ACCOUNTS PAYABLE (CONTROL)		GENERAL LEDGER				GL 7
					Balance	
Date	Item	Post	Debit	Credit	Debit	Credit
EOM		PJ 1		C 3,500		

Note that the accounts payable column in the purchase journal is posted twice, the total and the intermediate items. The total is posted to the general ledger and the intermediate items in the same column are posted to the accounts payable ledger. This double posting is because the total is used in the accounting process by the accountant and the intermediate items are not part of the accounting process and are used by management only.

Item B. The purchase journal records the items that are purchased on credit. The accounts payable column describes who is owed the money for the purchases. Then the numbers in the accounts payable column are extended in order to show the type of items being purchased. The extended columns could be headed, sub contract, supplies, lodging etc. The total of each of the extended items are posted to the general ledger. In this case the only extension was to purchases, the total of which must be posted to page GL 52 of the general ledger.

The amount posted to the accounts payable page of the general ledger (GL 7) ($3,500) must equal the combined amount posted to the subsidiary ledger ($1,400 + $1,200 + $900). See Item C below.

From the purchases column in the purchase journal, the total ($3,500, a debit) is posted to the purchases page of the general ledger (GL 52) as a debit. Note the indicated source of the posting, PJ 1.

PURCHASES			GENERAL LEDGER		GL	52
					Balance	
Date	Item	Post	Debit	Credit	Debit	Credit
EOM		PJ 1	A 3,500			

Note. The first two posting (Items A and B above) are examples of the double-entry system of accounting.

There is a debit and credit of $3,500. Theoretically the there is no need of further posting. But, as of the moment, the names of the creditors, the amount owed, and when payments are due are not displayed. This information is supplied by the use of a subsidiary ledger.

Item C. The following three pages in the accounts payable ledger illustrate the posting of the intermediate items (shown in italic type) to the accounts payable ledgers. Note the "post" columns of the purchase journal displays the destination of the posting and the "post" column in the accounts payable ledger indicates the source of the posting.

The intermediate items (credits) from the purchase journal are individually posted to the accounts payable subsidiary ledger, as a credit, as shown below. The accounts payable ledger has a page number for each creditor. Note the indicated source of the postings, *PJ 1*, a third time.

Vender Name	Destination	Amount
Comet Co.	AP C	1,400
Asteroid Co.	AP A	1,200
Nebula Co.	AP N	900

ACCOUNTS PAYABLE LEDGER						
Name: **COMET CO.**			*Terms:* NET 30			**AP C**
Date	Item		Post	Debit	Credit	Balance
EOM			PJ 1		B 1,400	

ACCOUNTS PAYABLE LEDGER

Name:	ASTEROID CO.		Terms:	2% 10 NET 30		AP A
Date	Item	Post	Debit	Credit	Balance
EOM		PJ 1		**_B_** *1,200*	

ACCOUNTS PAYABLE LEDGER

Name:	NEBULA CO.		Terms:	2% 10 NET 30		AP N
Date	Item	Post	Debit	Credit	Balance
EOM		PJ 1		**_B_** *900*	

In the purchase journal (Figure 2-6 above), it can be seen the total of the accounts payable column and the total of the purchase column are posted to the general ledger. The totals are posted to the general ledger because "totals" are used in the accounting process. Intermediate items are not posted to the general ledger because intermediate items are only used for informative purposes.

Note. All of the intermediate items are posted to the accounts payable ledger as credits. They are posted as credits because accounts payable, the heading of the column, is a credit. Subsidiary ledgers are posted using the same denomination as the column total. When the column totals are credits the posting to the subsidiary ledger are also credits. Logically, the total of the accounts payable column is a credit and all components of the accounts payable should also be credits

All of the intermediate items are posted to the accounts payable ledger by the use of the single-entry system of accounting. Observe the accounts payable column in Figure 2-6, the total of the column is posted to the general ledger. The intermediate items are the numbers that make up the total. The intermediate items describe the total. The intermediate items are the foundation of the total. The total has already been posted and posting of the intermediate items would result in double posting.

Helpful Tip The double-entry system of accounting is used when entering and posting to and from the journals and ledgers. There is, however, an exception. The single-entry system is used when posting *intermediate items* (see Item C above). For example, the *accounts payable* column in the purchase journal is posted twice, the total ($3,500) and the intermediate items (totaling $3,500). The total is posted to the general ledger and the *intermediate items* in the same column are posted to the accounts payable ledger. This additional posting is because the total is used in the accounting process by the accountant and is part of the double-entry system, but the intermediate items are not part of the accounting process and so a single-entry system is all that is required. A single entry to a subsidiary ledger creates a tool for use by management.

The Purchase Journal following the purchase of stars is shown in Figure 2-8 below.

Figure 2-8. Diagram of Purchase Journal and Ledgers Following Purchase of Stars

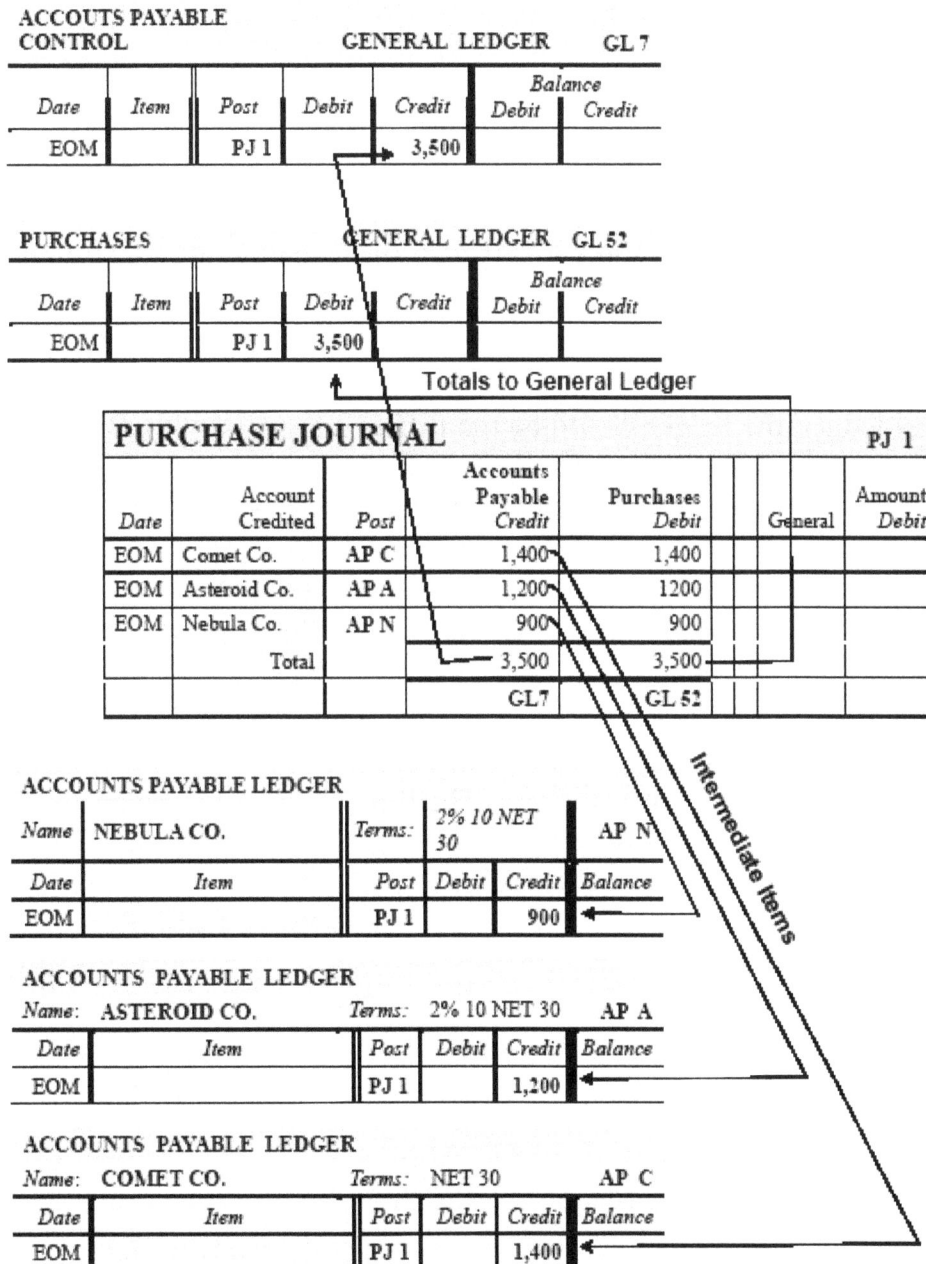

ACCOUNTS PAYABLE
CONTROL   GENERAL LEDGER   GL 7

Date	Item	Post	Debit	Credit	Balance Debit	Balance Credit
EOM		PJ 1		3,500		

PURCHASES   GENERAL LEDGER   GL 52

Date	Item	Post	Debit	Credit	Balance Debit	Balance Credit
EOM		PJ 1	3,500			

Totals to General Ledger

PURCHASE JOURNAL   PJ 1

Date	Account Credited	Post	Accounts Payable Credit	Purchases Debit	General	Amount Debit
EOM	Comet Co.	AP C	1,400	1,400		
EOM	Asteroid Co.	AP A	1,200	1200		
EOM	Nebula Co.	AP N	900	900		
	Total		3,500	3,500		
			GL7	GL 52		

ACCOUNTS PAYABLE LEDGER

Name	NEBULA CO.		Terms:	2% 10 NET 30		AP N

Date	Item	Post	Debit	Credit	Balance
EOM		PJ 1		900	

ACCOUNTS PAYABLE LEDGER

Name:	ASTEROID CO.		Terms:	2% 10 NET 30	AP A

Date	Item	Post	Debit	Credit	Balance
EOM		PJ 1		1,200	

ACCOUNTS PAYABLE LEDGER

Name:	COMET CO.		Terms:	NET 30	AP C

Date	Item	Post	Debit	Credit	Balance
EOM		PJ 1		1,400	

Intermediate Items

Helpful Tip. It is good accounting practice when posting from a journal to post the totals of the columns first, then to post the general column (if there are any items), and to post the intermediate items (if there are any) last. Thus, as shown in Figure 2-8, the total of the *accounts payable column* in the Purchase Journal is posted to GL 7; the total of the *purchase column* in the Purchase Journal is posted to GL 52; and the intermediate items are posted to their individual page in the Accounts Payable Ledger. There were no items in the general column to be posted.

A. Function of the Subsidiary Ledger

As previously mentioned, the major function of a subsidiary ledger is to inform management as to specific detail of transactions. In the case of the Star Company, for example, subsidiary ledgers inform management of the names and other details of the businesses that owe Star Company money, the names and other details of the businesses to which Star Company owes money, and who received commissions and how much.

Frequently, the details of a transaction are needed. If all of the details were combined in the general ledger, the ledger would be too difficult to work with. By keeping the details and individual transaction amounts shown in a subsidiary ledger, the underlying information (details of a transaction) can be accessed (by date). When the total of the individual transactions shown in the journal are posted to the general ledger, only the total amount is recorded, but the underlying details (dates, amounts, and so on) are not known. By knowing the detail of each sale, the details of each purchase, and the details of each commission recipient—which are stored in subsidiary ledgers—management is able to make decisions rapidly.

The Star Company maintains 3 subsidiary ledgers. The subsidiary ledgers are controlled by 3 pages in the general ledger. The three general ledger control accounts and their subsidiary ledgers are as follows:

General Ledger Account		Subsidiary Ledger Account
Accounts Payable (Control) (GL 7)	→	Accounts Payable Subsidiary Ledger
Accounts Receivable (Control) (GL 3)	→	Accounts Receivable Subsidiary Ledger
Commission (Control) (GL 54)	→	Commission Subsidiary Ledger

The general ledger *control* account consists only of the "totals" and the subsidiary ledger accounts can have many transactions. For example, if 50 sales were made on credit and each sale was paid for at the same time, the *total* amount of money received would be recorded in the accounts receivable page of the general ledger. Without a subsidiary ledger, 50 recordations would have to be made to the general ledger. By establishing subsidiary ledgers, the general ledger remains small and manageable. The general ledger is in charge and controls the underlying subsidiary ledger. Before a trial balance can be made, the accounting department must verify that the totals in the subsidiary ledgers are in agreement with the totals shown in the general ledger.

Helpful Tip. The accounts payable (subsidiary) ledger and the accounts payable general ledger (GL 7) are in essence the same account, but are located in different books of account. Similarly, the accounts receivable (subsidiary) ledger and the accounts receivable general ledger (GL 3), and the commission (subsidiary) ledger and the commission general ledger (GL 54), are also the same account, but located in different books of account. Thus, accounts payable ledger is controlled by the general ledger (GL 7); the accounts receivable ledger is controlled by the general ledger (GL 3); and the commission ledger is controlled by the general ledger (GL 54).

B. Observations

➢ One of the main purposes of subsidiary ledgers is to reduce the number of pages in the general ledger.

➢ Subsidiary ledgers also inform management of the names and other details of the businesses which owe Star Company money, the names and other details of the businesses to which Star Company owes money and who received commission and how much. The information stored in a subsidiary ledger is used when management decides to pay a bill, a commission, or wishes to find out who and how much money is owed to the business.

➢ Single-entry accounting occurs when only one part of a journal entry is posted. If a debit is posted there is no credit. If a credit is posted there is no debit. The single-entry system is employed only when posting intermediate items to a subsidiary ledger.

➢ The totals of all the accounts from journals are always posted to the general ledger. For example, the total of the *accounts payable* column ($3,500) is posted to the general ledger (GL 7) control account.

➢ The intermediate items are always posted to subsidiary ledgers. For example, the intermediate items shown in the *accounts payable* column ($1,400, $1,200, and $900) are posted to the accounts payable (subsidiary) ledger for use by management.

➢ The general ledger shows the total and the subsidiary ledger contains an itemization of the total.

- ➢ Intermediate items are always of the same denomination as that of the column total. Thus, if the column total is a debit, the intermediate items are debits; if the column total is a credit, the intermediate items are credits.

- ➢ Each of the three subsidiary ledgers stands by itself and has no relationship to any of the other books except for its corresponding page in the general ledger.

- ➢ Before a trial balance can be made, the accounting department must verify that the totals in the subsidiary ledgers are in agreement with the totals shown in the general ledger. For example, the total of all the amounts in the accounts payable *ledger* must always be in mathematical agreement with the accounts payable *page* of the general ledger.

- ➢ The general ledger account and the subsidiary ledger are interdependent. One records the total and the other the details. In both cases, the source for the information one of the four journals. For example, the source of the posting to the general ledger for purchases and to the subsidiary ledger for purchases is the same, that is, both originated from the *accounts payable column* of the purchase journal. They differ in that the total of the accounts payable column is posted to the general ledger and the intermediate items are posted to the accounts payable subsidiary ledger.

- ➢

4. THE CHECK DISBURSEMENT JOURNAL

All businesses issue checks to pay for goods and services purchased on credit. Later these checks are recorded in the check disbursement journal as part of the accounting process.

The check disbursement journal is usually a large sheet of columnar paper typically similar to the one shown below in Figure 2-9 below. The column with the heading "Bank," is the master column. Each check listed under the bank column is extended to the column whose heading best describes the purpose for which it was issued. The total of the column headed bank must equal the combined sum of the remaining columns. At the end of the accounting period the columns are totaled and cross footed in order to assure mathematical accuracy.

Chapter 1 was designed to instruct the student in the basics of accounting, the nomenclature, the trial balance, and the balance sheet and profit and loss statement through the use of journal entries. In this chapter, all transactions of Star Company are being recorded through accounting books.

The authors suggest that each of the transactions listed below be observed from the following perspective:

➤ See how the transactions are recorded in the check disbursement journal.

➤ Study the extensions and how they are placed under specific columnar headings.

➤ Study the chart of accounts and understand how it is used to direct posting to the general ledger.

➤ Observe the "general" column in Figure 2-9 below and note how the individual items are posted to the general ledger, but the column total is not.

Note. The transactions used in this section are the same as the journal entries recorded in Chapter 1.

In chapter 1 there were sixteen transactions. The transactions that affected "Bank" are as follows:

Transaction # 3

Star Company issues check #101 in the amount of $60 to Seaside Telephone for phone usage.

Transaction # 5

Star Company issues check #102 for $200 in order to set up a petty-cash fund to be used to repay employees for cash expended by employees on behalf of the company.

Transaction # 6

Star Company issues check #103 in the amount of $1,100 to Jackson Furniture for the purchase of furniture and fixtures.

Transaction # 7

Star Company gives check #104 for $1,500 to Edgar Motors to pay for a truck to be used in the business.

Transaction # 9

Star Company issues check #105 in the amount of $500 to repay a portion of the $5,000 loan due to Alpine Bank.

Transaction # 11

Star Company gives check #106 to Fern Rentals in the amount of $1,500 for the payment of the current month's rent ($500), and a deposit of $1,000 for the last two months of a five year lease.

Transaction # 12

Star Company issues checks (#107, #108, and #109) for commission as follows:
John Roberts - $450
Robert Brown - $600
Stanley Steel - $500

Transaction # 13

Mr. Jones, the owner of Star Co, requests funds for his own personal use. Star Company issues check #110 for $800 to Mr. Jones.

Transaction # 14

Star Company issues check #111 for $1,400 to Comet to pay off its debt, thereby reducing accounts payable.

The transactions shown above were all entered in the check disbursement journal; see Figure 2-9. The Transaction number for each check written is indicated in the first column of the check disbursement journal.

Figure 2-9. Completed Check Disbursement Journal

CHECK DISBURSEMENT JOURNAL											CD 1
Tran No	Payee	Check No.	Bank Credit	Comm-ission Debit	Telephone Debit	Rent Debit	Petty Cash Debit	Owner's Equity Debit	Accounts Payable Debit	Explanation	General Debit
3	Seaside Tel.	101	60		60						
5	Petty Cash	102	200				200				
6	Jo's Furniture	103	1,100							*E GL5 Equipment-F&F*	*1,100*
7	Edgar Motors	104	1,500							*E GL5 Equipment-Truck*	*1,500*
9	Alpine Bank	105	500							*F GL8 Loan Pay. Alpine Bank*	*500*
11	Fern Rentals	106	1,500			500				*G GL4 Deposit-Rent*	*1,000*
12	John Roberts	107	450	*CL R K 450*							
12	Robert Brown	108	600	*CL B K 600*							
12	Stanley Steel	109	500	*CL S K 500*							
13	Mr. Jones	110	800					800			
14	Comet Co.	111	1,400						*AP C I 1,400*		
		Totals:	8,610	1,550	60	500	200	800	1,400		4,100
			GL 1	GL 54	GL 57	GL56	GL 2	GL 9	GL 7		
			A	*J*	*B*	*B*	*C*	*D*	*H*		No!

Note. The letters and numbers in italic type are explained below. Other postings and balances are also shown.

Keep the following in mind; they apply to all Journals.

- The total of all columns are posted to the general ledger

- The items in the general column are posted to the general ledger

- The intermediate items in columns with the headings accounts payable, accounts receivable, and commission are posted to subsidiary ledgers

- The total of the general column is only used for cross-footing purposes. It is never posted.

In the following explanations, the totals of all the columns in Figure 2-9 (except the general column) will be posted to the general ledger. The total of the general column ($4,100) is only used for cross-footing purposes (explained later). The intermediate items (K and I) are posted individually to the subsidiary ledgers. The following is a discussion of the postings.

Note. All postings of the check disbursement journal are keyed off to correspond with the ledgers to which they are being posted. For example, "GL 1" represents the account *bank* in the general ledger. See Figure 2-3, *Chart of Accounts*.

Posting *A* for $8,610 to Record Total Cash Disbursed

From the *bank* column in the check disbursement journal, the total ($8,610, a *credit*) is posted as a *credit* to the account *bank* in the *general ledger* (GL1). The source of the posting is shown in the *post* column of the general ledger. CD 1 (in the upper right corner of the Check Disbursement Journal) stands for check disbursement journal, page 1.

The *general ledger* contains a page for each item listed on the *chart of accounts*. The general ledger for the Star Company has only 19 pages in the *general ledger.* A general ledger could contain many pages, each page representing a different account. When additional space is needed on a page, an additional *continuation* sheet is merely inserted **in front of (or behind)** an existing page; the general ledger page number does *not* change.

Purpose: to keep a record of the money the business has in the bank. See Figure 2-9, *Completed Check Disbursement Journal.*

BANK		GENERAL LEDGER				GL 1	
						Balance	
Date	Item	Post	Debit	Credit	Debit	Credit
EOM		CR 1	10,500			
EOM		*CD 1*		*A 8,610*	1,890	

Disbursing company funds ($8,610) is bad for the business and is entered as a *credit.* The balance of $1,890 ($10,500 - $8,610), an asset, is entered as a *debit* and posted to the Trial Balance.

Posting B for $60 Telephone and $500 Rent Expenses

The amounts in the *telephone* and *rent* columns of the *check disbursement journal* ($60 and $500, both *debits*) are posted as *debits* to their respective accounts in the *general ledger*. The general ledger page numbers are ascertained by referring to the *Chart of Accounts* (see Figure 2-3). The two postings are displayed below. [See Figure 2-9 and Transactions #3 and #11]

Purpose: to keep record of the money paid for telephone and rent expenses.

TELEPHONE		GENERAL LEDGER			GL 57	
					Balance	
Date	Item	Post	Debit	Credit	Debit	Credit
EOM		PC 1	10		10	
EOM		*CD 1*	*B 60*		70	

Purpose: to keep record of the money paid for rent expense.

RENT		GENERAL LEDGER			GL 56	
					Balance	
Date	Item	Post	Debit	Credit	Debit	Credit
EOM		*CR 1*	*B 500*		500	

Both *rent* and *telephone* are expenses that affect profit and loss. All expenses are *debits*.

Posting C for $200 to Create a Petty Cash Fund

From the *petty cash* column of the *check disbursement journal*, $200 (a *debit*) is posted as a *debit* to the petty cash account of the *general ledger (GL 2)*. [See Figure 2-9 and Transactions #5]

Purpose: to keep record of the amount of money in the petty cash account.

PETTY CASH		GENERAL LEDGER			GL 2	
					Balance	
Date	Item	Post	Debit	Credit	Debit	Credit
EOM		*CD 1*	*C 200*			
EOM	Due petty cash fund	PC 1		190	10	

Having more money in the *petty cash* account, a balance-sheet item is a *debit*.

Posting D for $800 Owner's Withdrawal

From the *owner's equity* column of the check disbursement journal, $800 (a *debit*) is posted as a *debit* to the *owner's equity* page of the *general ledger,* GL 9.

The owner's equity is the sum of the amount the owner has invested from his personal funds and the accumulated profit of the business, less accumulated (previous) losses of the business and the amount of money the owner has withdrawn from the business. The $800 withdrawal merely reduces the owner's equity in the business. The withdrawal has no affect on profit or loss.

Purpose: to keep an ongoing record of the owner's net worth. [See Figure 2-9 and Transaction #13]

| OWNER'S EQUITY | | GENERAL LEDGER | | | GL 9 | |
Date	Item	Post	Debit	Credit	Balance Debit	Balance Credit
EOM		CD 1		4,000		
EOM		*CD 1*	*D 800*			3,200

Note. *Owner's equity*, a balance-sheet item, is reflected as a *credit* on the balance sheet when assets exceed liabilities. The account is *debited* to reflect the $800 reduction in *owner's equity* (or net worth).

Posting E for $1,500 and $1,100 Purchases of Equipment

From the *general* column of the *check disbursement journal*, both the amount of equipment purchased ($1,500 and $1,100, both *debits*) are posted to the equipment page of the *general ledger*, GL5, as *debits*.

Purpose: to keep a record of the cost of the equipment owned by the business. [See Figure 2-9 and Transactions #6 and #7]

| EQUIPMENT | | GENERAL LEDGER | | | GL 5 | |
Date	Item	Post	Debit	Credit	Balance Debit	Balance Credit
EOM	Furniture & Fixtures	*CD 1*	*E 1,100*			
	Acq. 1/1/11, Life 8 years					
EOM	Truck, 2009 Rawley	*CD 1*	*E 1,500*			
	Acq. 1/1/11, Life 5 years				2,600	

Note. A total of $2,600 in equipment was purchased. The cost of equipment is really an expense and rightfully belongs in profit and loss. The government agrees that it is an expense, but the tax laws only permit business to write off the cost of the equipment over the life of the equipment.

In accounting, there is only one way to meet the requirements of business and the government; the equipment must be treated as if it were a capital asset. In this way the cost of the equipment remains on the books and is depreciated over its life. Thus, if a piece of equipment costs $5,000 and has a 5-year life, $1,000 can be expensed. After taking the expense of $1,000 in the current year, assuming the purchase is made at the beginning of the accounting year, the account would appear as follows on the balance sheet:

	Debit	*Credit*
Equipment	5,000	
Reserve for depreciation		1,000

The balance sheet is ever changing, but lasts throughout the life of the business. Thus there is always a record maintained of the equipment cost, and how much it has been depreciated. In each succeeding year, a $1,000 expense may be taken until such time the cost ($5,000) is written off. This type of depreciation is known as "straight line." Other types of depreciation methods may be used (e.g., accelerated depreciation). A record of the amount of depreciation is kept on a separate page in the *general ledger* having an account name *reserve for depreciation* (GL 6).

Posting *F* for $500 Repayment of Loan

From the *general* column of the *check disbursement journal,* $500 (a *debit*) is posted as a *debit* to the *loans payable* page of the *general ledger* (GL8).

Helpful Tip. The loan payable account is kept in the general ledger because Star Company does not intend borrow additional funds. In the event Star Company contemplated borrowing more funds, the accounting department could create a subsidiary ledger, a Loans Payable Ledger.

The $500 is a reduction of a loan. The original loan of $5,000 (also shown) is reduced to $4,500 after the repayment is made.

Purpose: to keep a record of the loan status. [See Figure 2-9 and Transaction #9]

LOANS PAYABLE		GENERAL LEDGER					GL 8
						Balance	
Date	Item	Post	Debit	Credit	Debit	Credit
EOM	Alpine Bank	CR 1		5,000		
EOM	Alpine Bank	CD 1	F 500			4,500

Posting G for $1,000 Rent Deposit

From the *general* column of the *check disbursement Journal,* $1,000 (a *debit*) is posted to the deposit page of the *general ledger*, GL 4, as a *debit*.

A deposit on rent, when given, is neither good nor bad. At the time of the deposit its fate is not known. The deposit might be returned or it might be applied to future rent. When the future of any item is unknown it is placed on the *balance sheet*.

Purpose: to keep a permanent record of the rent deposit. [See Figure 2-9 and Transaction #11]

DEPOSITS		GENERAL LEDGER					GL 4
						Balance	
Date	Item	Post	Debit	Credit	Debit	Credit
EOM	Rent-Fenway Rentals	CD 1	G 1,000		1,000	

Posting H for $1,400 Reduction of Account Payable

From the accounts payable column of the check disbursement journal, $1,400 (a debit) is posted to the general ledger as a debit.

Purpose: to keep a record of the total amount of money owed for merchandise which Star Company purchased on credit. The amount of money owed is decreased by $1,400. [See Figure 2-9 and Transaction #14]

ACCOUNTS PAYABLE (CONTROL)		GENERAL LEDGER					GL 7
						Balance	
Date	Item	Post	Debit	Credit	Debit	Credit
EOM		CD 1	H 1,400			

Posting _I_ for $1,400 to Record Customer Payment to the Accounts Payable Subsidiary Ledger

From the *accounts* payable column of the *check disbursement journal*, the intermediate amount ($1,400, a *debit)* is posted as a *debit* in the *accounts payable ledger,* a subsidiary ledger.

Purpose: to record a customer payment. [See Figure 2-9 and Transaction #14]

ACCOUNTS PAYABLE LEDGER

Name: **COMET CO.**		Terms: NET 30				AP C
Date	Item		Post	Debit	Credit	Balance
EOM			*CD 1*	*I 1,400*		

Posting _J_ for $1,550 for Commissions Paid

From the *commission* column of the check disbursement journal, the total amount of commission paid ($1,550, a *debit)* is posted as a *debit* to the *general ledger*.

Purpose: to record in the general ledger the total amount of commission paid. [See Figure 2-9 and Transaction #12]

COMMISSION (CONTROL)   **GENERAL LEDGER**   **GL   54**

Date	Item	Post	Debit	Credit	Balance	
					Debit	Credit
EOM		*CR 1*	*J 1,550*		1,550	

Posting _K_ for $450, $600, and $500 for Commissions Paid

In the books of Star Company the *commission ledger is* a subsidiary ledger.

From the commission column of the *check disbursement journal, $450, $600,* and *$500* (all *debits)* are posted to the John Roberts, Robert Brown and Stanley Steel pages in the *Commission ledger* as debits. [See Figure 2-9 and Transaction #12]

Note. The total of commission paid was previously recorded into the commission page of the general ledger. An itemization as to who was paid the commission is recorded in the subsidiary commission ledgers, as shown below.

Name	BROWN, ROBERT	COMMISSION LEDGER			CL B	
					Balance	
Date	Item	Post	Debit	Credit	Debit	Credit
EOM		CD 1	K 600		600	

Name	ROBERTS, JOHN	COMMISSION LEDGER			CL R	
					Balance	
Date	Item	Post	Debit	Credit	Debit	Credit
EOM		CD 1	K 450		450	

Name:	STEEL, STANLEY	COMMISSION LEDGER			CL S	
					Balance	
Date	Item	Post	Debit	Credit	Debit	Credit
EOM		CD 1	K 500		500	

Consider only the column headed "Commission" in Figure 2-9, *Completed Check Disbursement Journal,* shown above. As each question is posed and answered please refer to Figure 2-9.

Q 1. What is posted to subsidiary ledgers?

All intermediate items in the column headed Commission

Q 2. What is an "intermediate Item?"

All numbers between the column heading and the column total.

Q 3. Why are intermediate items posted to subsidiary ledgers?

The subsidiary ledgers keep track of the details regarding each transaction. For example, the commission earned by Roberts, Brown, and Steel shown in the commission column are posted to their pages in the subsidiary ledger.

Q 4. Why is the total of the Commission column, $1,550, posted to the General Ledger and not to the Commission Ledger?

The General Ledger keeps a record of the "totals." The Commission Ledger keeps track how much each commission recipient earned.

Q 5. **If the total of the commission column has already been posted to the General Ledger, why do we need a subsidiary ledger to record who earned the commission?**

The totals are posted to the general ledger, but management needs to know information that is only found in the subsidiary ledgers, such as:

- Who earned the commission and the amount that was earned
- To whom Star Company sold merchandise, how much is receivable, the terms, and so on
- From whom did Star Company buy merchandise, how much is payable, the terms, and so on.

Observations

➤ The totals of all the columns, except the general column, are posted to the *general ledger.*

➤ The total of the general column is only used for cross-footing purposes (and is never posted), but the intermediate items in that column are posted individually to the *general ledger.*

➤ After the posting of all column totals and the items in the general column, the only numbers left in the check disbursement journal to be posted are the intermediate items.

➤ All numbers between the column heading and the column total are called intermediate items. The intermediate items in the columns with the headings accounts receivable, accounts payable, and commission are all posted to their respective subsidiary ledgers. The intermediate items in the other columns are for convenience. For example, if wages of $500 was paid once a week, the total of $2,000 is posted to the general ledger, but the intermediate four items of $500 are of no consequence.

➤ When the future of any item is unknown it is placed on the *balance sheet.*

➤ The intermediate items in the commission column (posting <u>K</u>) are posted to the Commission Ledger.

➤ The intermediate items in the accounts payable column (posting <u>I</u>) are posted to the Accounts Payable Ledger.

➤ Accounting uses the check disbursement journal to summarize repetitive transactions.

5. Creating a Check Disbursement Journal from the Checking Account

A *check disbursement journal* is created from the business's checking account, as follows:

1. Using the check stubs, enter the check number, names of the payees, and the amounts paid into the *check disbursement journal* (see below).

2. Extend each check amount to the column with the headings that best describes its purpose.

   Note. If none of the columns are suitable, enter the amount in the *general* column with a brief explanation.

CHECK DISBURSEMENT JOURNAL											CD 1
Tran No	Payee	Check No.	Bank Credit	Commission Debit	Tele-phone Debit	Rent Debit	Petty Cash Debit	Owner Equity Debit	Accounts Payable Debit	Explanation	General Debit

3. Add the columns.

4. Cross-foot the columns. To *cross foot* means to verify that the sum of the totals in all other columns agree with the total of the master column. For example, in Figure 2-9 above, the total of the bank column ($8,610) must be the same as the sum of the remaining columns (including the sum of the general column). If the amounts agree, a small check mark is placed next to the total in the master column.

$$\$8,610 = \$1,550 + \$60 + \$500 + \$200 + \$800 + \$1,400 + 4,100$$

5. Refer to the *chart of accounts* and enter the *general ledger* (GL) page numbers to which the totals are to be posted.

6. Post the totals of all the columns, including accounts receivable, accounts payable, and the commission columns, into the correct pages in the general ledger.

7. Post the items in the general column into the general ledger.

8. Post intermediate items to subsidiary ledgers.

6. Student Exercise

The following exercise is designed to enable the student to practice what has been explained in this segment of the book; that is, posting from the check disbursement journal to the general and subsidiary ledgers.

For this exercise:

- The Chart of Accounts is displayed.

- The Check Disbursement Journal, as well as all the necessary ledgers, are shown ready to receive the postings.

- Using the check disbursement journal that follows, post all of the relevant items to their respective ledgers.

- The posting symbols for intermediate items are shown.

- If necessary, review the previous section, which explains how the postings should be made.

- When posting intermediate item to the accounts payable subsidiary ledger use symbol *AP plus* the first letter of the last name to signify to which page the intermediate item is posted.

- When posting intermediate items to the accounts receivable subsidiary ledger use symbol *AR plus* the first letter of the last name.

- When posting intermediate items to the commission subsidiary ledger use symbol *CL plus* the first letter of the last name.

The Chart of Accounts and Check Disbursement Journal for this exercise are shown below. The transaction numbers are shown in the left column.

Helpful Tip. The totals are posted first to the general ledger and then the intermediate items are posted to the subsidiary ledger.

General Ledger Chart of Accounts

Balance Sheet Items	GL #	Profit and Loss Items	GL #
Accounts Payable (Control)	7	Auto Expense	53
Accounts Receivable (Control)	3	Commission (Control)	54
Bank	1	Food and Lodging	55
Deposits	4	Depreciation	58
Inventory	10	Profit & Loss	59
Loans Payable	8	Purchases	52
Owner's Equity	9	Rent	56
Equipment	5	Telephone	57
Petty Cash	2	Sales	51
Reserve for Depreciation	6		

CHECK DISBURSEMENT JOURNAL · CD 1

Tran No	Payee	Check No.	Bank Credit	Comm-ission Debit	Tele-phone Debit	Rent Debit	Petty Cash Debit	Owner Equity Debit	Accounts Payable Debit	Explanation	General Debit
3	Seaside Tel	101	60		60						
5	Petty Cash	102	200				200				
6	Jo's Furniture	103	1,100							__Equip-ment F&F	1,100
7	Edgar Motors	104	1,500							__Equip-ment Truck	1,500
9	Alpine Bank	105	500							__Loan Payable Alpine Bank	500
11	Fred Rentals	106	1,500				500			__Deposit-Rent	1,000
12	John Roberts	107	450	__ 450							
12	Robert Brown	108	600	__ 600							
12	Stanley Steel	109	500	__ 500							
13	Mr. Jones	110	800					800			
14	Comet Co.	111	1,400						__ 1,400		
		Total	8,610	1,550	60	500	200	800	1,400		4,133
			GL __	GL __	GL __	GL __	GL __	GL __	GL __		

Be sure to cross-foot the above columns before proceeding.

$_____ = $_____ + $_____ + $_____ + $_____ + $_____ + $_____ + $_____

Did the amounts cross-foot? If the amounts do not cross-foot, it will be necessary to find and the error in the check disbursement journal before proceeding.

The general ledgers for this exercise are shown below.

BANK		GENERAL LEDGER					GL 1
						Balance	
Date	Item	Post	Debit	Credit	Debit	Credit	
EOM		CD 1					

PETTY CASH		GENERAL LEDGER					GL 2
						Balance	
Date	Item	Post	Debit	Credit	Debit	Credit	
EOM		CD 1					

DEPOSITS		GENERAL LEDGER					GL 4
						Balance	
Date	Item	Post	Debit	Credit	Debit	Credit	
EOM	Rent-Fenway Rentals	CD 1					

EQUIPMENT		GENERAL LEDGER					GL 5
						Balance	
Date	Item	Post	Debit	Credit	Debit	Credit	
EOM	Furniture & Fixtures	CD 1					
	Acq. 1/1/11, Life 8 years						
EOM	Truck, 2009 Rawley	CD 1					
	Acq. 1/1/11, Life 5 years						

ACCOUNTS PAYABLE (CONTROL)

GENERAL LEDGER

GL 7

Date	Item	Post	Debit	Credit	Balance Debit	Balance Credit
EOM		CD 1				

LOANS PAYABLE

GENERAL LEDGER

GL 8

Date	Item	Post	Debit	Credit	Balance Debit	Balance Credit
EOM	Alpine Bank	CD 1				

OWNER'S EQUITY

GENERAL LEDGER

GL 9

Date	Item	Post	Debit	Credit	Balance Debit	Balance Credit
EOM		CD 1				

COMMISSION

GENERAL LEDGER

GL 54

Date	Item	Post	Debit	Credit	Balance Debit	Balance Credit
EOM		CD 1				

RENT

GENERAL LEDGER

GL 56

Date	Item	Post	Debit	Credit	Balance Debit	Balance Credit
EOM		CD 1				

TELEPHONE			GENERAL LEDGER				GL 57
					Balance		
Date	Item	Post	Debit	Credit	Debit	Credit	
EOM		CD 1					
EOM		PC 1					

The subsidiary ledgers for this exercise are shown below.

Name	ROBERTS, JOHN		COMMISSION LEDGER				CL R
					Balance		
Date	Item	Post	Debit	Credit	Debit	Credit	
EOM		CD 1					

Name	STEEL, STANLEY		COMMISSION LEDGER				CL S
					Balance		
Date	Item	Post	Debit	Credit	Debit	Credit	
EOM		CD 1					

Name	BROWN, ROBERT		COMMISSION LEDGER				CL B
					Balance		
Date	Item	Post	Debit	Credit	Debit	Credit	
EOM		CD 1					

ACCOUNTS PAYABLE LEDGER						AP C
Name: COMET COMPANY		Terms: NET 30				
Date	Item	Post	Debit	Credit	Balance	
EOM		CD 1				

7. Bank Reconciliation

Each time a bank statement is received, the balance shown on the bank statement, reduced by the outstanding checks, should be compared to the balance in the check book. Comparison of the two balances, and correcting errors when necessary, is called bank reconciliation. See Section 8, *Finding Errors*, below.

In the past, the bank statement arrived with all the cleared checks listed on the statement and all cancelled checks enclosed. Now they arrive with pictures of cleared checks, and in some cases, no cancelled checks enclosed. In the explanation that follows, it will be assumed there are no cancelled checks enclosed with the checking account statement.

1. Locate and number consecutively (starting with #1) every minus amount in the areas where deposits and cancelled checks are listed on the bank statement.

2. Assume there is a list of outstanding checks from the previous month and that the current month's checks are listed, extended, totaled, and cross-footed in the check disbursement journal.

3. The term "outstanding checks" means those checks issued by the business that have not, as yet, been paid by the bank nor listed on the bank statement.

4. Starting with #1 on the bank statement, find that specific check among the outstanding checks or among the current checks in your check disbursement journal. To the right of the outstanding or current check mark "#1" and *circle the number on the bank statement.*

5. Later, if there is a minus number on the bank statement not circled, find out why. It could be an unrecorded check, or a legitimate bank charge, and so on. If it is a bank error, record the situation in the current months check listing and mark "bank error" in the general column to be sure of reimbursement.

6. Among the checks outstanding and among the current month's checks there will be checks that have no number next to them on the bank statement indicating they are outstanding. Make a small circle, preferably in red pencil, next to the unnumbered checks. Keep drawing circles through to the end of the accounting period.

7. List and total all the checks that have circles next to them. The total amount of these checks is what is referred to as *checks outstanding*.

8. List and total all deposits made through the end of the accounting period that are not reflected on the bank statement. The total of deposits that do not appear on the bank statement must be added to "balance per bank." For example, in the illustration below, the amount shown next to "Deposits outstanding" is $0. If there had been a $1,000 deposit made which does not show on the bank statement, the $1,000 figure

would be added to the Balance per bank. This would make the *balance per checkbook* be $5,500, instead of $4,500.

The two accounts are reconciled when the check book balance is $4,500, computed as follows:

Balance per bank (assumed)	$5,750
Plus Deposits outstanding	$0
Minus Checks outstanding (assumed)	- 1,250
Balance per checkbook	$4,500

If the check book shows a balance other than $4,500, either you or the bank has made an error. In all probability it is the banks error! But just to play it safe, be sure the deposits are in agreement, check the addition, check that your checks are not over or understated, and be sure all the minus figures on the bank statement are circled. Keep looking for the discrepancy until the balance per book equals $4,500.

8. Finding Errors

Errors generally follow one of several patterns. Here are some typical error patterns and what to do about them. Compute the difference, that is, the amount out of balance.

1. **Transposition (error divisible by 9).** When the difference between what you have and what you should have (expected balance) is evenly divisible by 9, you may have a transposition error. For example, take a number (say 64) and write it backwards (46). The difference of 18 (64 minus 46) is divisible by nine; possibly indicating that it is the result of a transposition error.

   The following method can be used to determine if a number is divisible by 9. If a number is divisible by 9, the sum of its digits, when *reduced to a single digit* will always equal 9. For example, take the number 2,997,000, is it divisible by 9?

   $$2 + 9 + 9 + 7 + 0 + 0 + 0 = 27$$

   $$2 + 7 = \underline{9} \text{ (thus, 2,997,000 is divisible by 9).}$$

2. **Number inclusion (or omission).** If the difference equals the amount of one of the entries, an amount was not included or included twice, and may be easy to find.

3. **Entry reversals (doubles and halves).** An entry reversal occurs when a *debit* is entered as a *credit* or a *credit* is entered as a *debit*. The difference will always be double the amount placed in the wrong column (or amounts were added that should have been subtracted, or vice versa). Check that amounts that are half of the difference are in the correct column.

4. **Keypad errors (3 or 3 x 10^n).** What if a column total is off by 3, 30, 300, or any multiple of 10? Each key on a ten-key pad of a computer or adding machine is exactly 3 higher than the key immediately below it. The four key is above the one key, the seven key is above the four key, and so on. In each case, the difference is always 3, 30, or 300, and so on, depending upon when the "hitting high" error occurred during the entry. Similarly, the difference can be -3, -30, or -300, and so on, by hitting too low during an entry. For example, assume "4000" is entered as "1000." A "hitting low" error may have occurred because the difference is 3,000.

9. The Cash Receipts Journal

The *cash receipts journal* is usually a large sheet of columnar paper typically similar to the one shown below. The first column, headed by the word "Bank," is the master column. The individual checks listed under *bank* are extended to the column whose heading best describes the reason they were received. The totals of the remaining columns (including the "General" column) must be equal to the total of the *bank* column. See Figure 2-10, *Completed Cash Receipts Journal,* below. At the end of the accounting period the columns are totaled and cross-footed in order to assure mathematical accuracy.

The student should study how the following transactions are entered into the cash receipts journal, the column headings, the extensions, and how and where the totals are posted. The following transactions will be used in this section and are the same as the journal entries recorded in Chapter 1. The transactions are as follows:

Transaction # 1

Mr. Jones starts a new business, Star Company, and he borrows $5,000 from the Alpine Bank which he deposits into the business checking account.

Transaction # 10

Mr. Jones withdraws $4,000 from his personal checking account and deposits the money into Star's Company's checking account to be used in the business.

Transaction # 15

Star Company deposits a $1,500 check from Mars reducing *accounts receivable.*

Figure 2-10. Completed Cash Receipts Journal

| CASH RECEIPTS JOURNAL | | | | | | | | | | | CR 1 |

Trans #		Bank Debit	Cash Sales Credit	Post	Accounts Receivable Credit	Post	Loans Payable Credit	Owner's Equity Credit	Explanation	General Credit
1	Alpine Bank	5,000					5,000			
10	M. Jones	4,000						4,000		
15	Mars Co.	1,500		*AR M*	*E* 1,500					
	Totals	*10,500*			*1,500*		*5,000*	*4,000*		
		GL 1			GL 3		GL 8	GL 9		
		A			*D*		*B*	*C*		

Note. The letters and numbers in italic type are explained below. Other postings and balances are also shown.

The totals of all the columns, except the *general* column, are posted to the *general ledger*. The total of the general column is only used for cross-footing purposes but the item amounts within the general column, if any, are posted individually to the *general ledger*.

Posting *A* to General Ledger

From the column headed *bank* in the *cash receipts journal*, $10,500 (a *debit*) is posted as a *debit* to the *bank* page in the *general ledger*, GL1. The source of the entry, CR 1, is entered in the "Post" column.

Purpose: the account Bank displays the total amount of money deposited and withdrawn during the accounting period. [See Figure 2-10]

BANK		GENERAL LEDGER					GL 1
						Balance	
Date	Item	Post	Debit	Credit		Debit	Credit
EOM		*CR 1*	*A* 10,500			10,500	

Posting _B_ to General Ledger (GL 8)

From the *loan payable* column of the *cash receipts journal* $5,000 is posted to loan payable page of the *general ledger GL 8*. [See Figure 2-10 and Transaction #1]

Businesses that have many loans would set up a subsidiary ledger, called the Loan Payable Ledger. Since Star Company contemplates having few loans it was deemed unnecessary.

Purpose: to keep a record of the names and amounts of money borrowed.

LOAN PAYABLE		GENERAL LEDGER			GL 8	
					Balance	
Date	Item	Post	Debit	Credit	Debit	Credit
EOM	Alpine Bank	CR 1		B 5,000		5,000

Posting _C_ to General Ledger (GL 9)

From the *owner's equity* column in the *cash receipts journal*, $4,000 is posted to the *owner's equity* page in the *general ledger*, GL 9. [See Figure 2-10 and Transaction #10]

"Owner's Equity" is the only account that is posted differently than all other accounts shown in the Chart of Accounts. When the owner of a business invests money, the balance sheet journal entry is from "good" (indicating an increase in the bank) to "good" (indicating an increase to the owner's equity) as shown in GL 9 below.

Owner's Equity is the book value of a business; it is equal to assets minus liabilities.

Purpose: to keep record of the owner's net worth.

OWNER'S EQUITY		GENERAL LEDGER			GL 9	
					Balance	
Date	Item	Post	Debit	Credit	Debit	Credit
EOM		CR 1		C 4,000		4,000
EOM		CD 1	800			3,200

Posting _D_ to General Ledger (GL 3)

From the *accounts receivable* column in the cash receipts journal, the $1,500 (a *credit*) is posted as a *credit* to the *accounts receivable control* page of the *general ledger*, GL3. The $1,500 was the total amount received as payment from all the customers of Star Company during this accounting period. [See Figure 2-10 and Transaction #15]

ACCOUNTS RECEIVABLE (CONTROL)		GENERAL LEDGER					GL 3
						Balance	
Date	Item	Post	Debit	Credit	Debit	Credit	
EOM		*CR 1*		_D_ *1,500*		1,500	

Posting _E_ to Subsidiary Ledger (AR M)

The total of the *accounts receivable* column ($1,500, a *credit*) is posted to the *general ledger* 'control' account, but the individual customer amounts (intermediate *credit* items) are posted as *credits* to the Accounts Receivable Ledger, a subsidiary ledger.

From the *accounts receivable* column of the *cash receipts journal*, the intermediate item ($1,500) is posted as a *credit* to the Mars Company page of the Accounts Receivable Ledger. [See Figure 2-10 and Transaction #15]

Purpose: to record payment by Mars Company reducing accounts receivable.

ACCOUNTS RECEIVABLE LEDGER					AR M
Name: **MARS COMPANY**.					
Date	Terms	Post	Debit	Credit	Balance
EOM		*CR 1*		_E_ *1,500*	1,500

A. Summary

The total of all the columns in the cash receipts journal has been posted to the general ledger a shown above. The posting of the totals form a journal entry, as summarized below.

Account Name	Letter	Account No.	Debit	Credit
Bank	A	GL1	10,500	
Accounts Receivable	B	GL3		1,500
Loans Payable	C	GL8		5,000
Owner's Equity	D	GL9		4,000

B. Observations

➢ All intermediate items are posted to subsidiary ledgers.

➢ The totals of all intermediate items are posted to the general ledger.

➢ Intermediate items and subsidiary ledgers form a separate set of books, the only connection being the *total* of the intermediate items are posted to the general ledger.

➢ Intermediate items are posted to subsidiary ledgers using the single-entry system of accounting.

➢ All receipts of money, no mater the source, are recorded into the cash receipts journal.

➢ The intermediate item in the loans payable column ($5,000) is not posted because they are not items that go into a subsidiary ledger. It was decided to place all loans and all loan reductions in the general ledger. If, on the other hand, it was anticipated there would be many loans, the accountant would set up a subsidiary ledger, the loans payable ledger. The loans total would be recorded in the general ledger and the intermediate items posted to the newly created loans payable (subsidiary) ledger.

➢ The $1,500 intermediate item in the accounts receivable column was posted (see Figure 2-10, *Completed Check Disbursement Journal*). Intermediate items are never posted unless a subsidiary ledger is involved. At present, only the accounts payable, accounts receivable, and commission columns are posted to subsidiary ledgers.

➤ All intermediate items in the accounts receivable column are posted to a subsidiary ledger, the accounts receivable ledger. All intermediate items in the accounts payable, accounts receivable and commission columns are posted to their subsidiary ledgers.

➤ The owner, Mr. Jones, can contribute as much as he likes and as often as he likes and only the total is relevant and is posted. See Figure 2-10.

10. The Purchase Journal and Accounts Payable (Control) Ledger

When purchases are made on credit, the total amount of the purchases is easy to record because the total is in the *purchase* column of the *purchase journal* (see Figure 2-11, *Completed Purchase Journal*, below). The total amount of money owed to all the creditors is also easy to record because it is clearly visible in the *accounts payable* column. The totals of all columns in the books of account are always posted to the General Ledger. Intermediate items in the accounts receivable, accounts payable, and commission columns ("subsidiary columns") are always posted to *subsidiary ledgers*. But it is imperative to remember, the totals of these columns are posted to the general ledger. The total of the intermediate items in the accounts payable column is equal to the total posted to the accounts payable page of the general ledger.

The *purchase journal* operates "hand-in-glove" with the *accounts payable* ledger because all purchases made on credit are recorded in the accounts payable column in the purchase journal and are posted to the accounts payable ledger. The purchase journal is typically similar to the one shown below (Figure 2-11 below). All purchases made on credit are listed in the purchase journal.

The total of all the pages in the *accounts payable ledger* must be equal to the total shown in the accounts payable page of *general ledger* (GL 7). Every creditor is assigned a separate page in the Accounts Payable Ledger. The *general ledger* keeps a record of the total owed and the subsidiary ledger keeps record of the creditors to whom money is owed. Each item in the *accounts payable* column of the *purchase journal* is extended to a column headed by the best descriptive caption. If no columns describe that specific type of expenditure, it is placed in the general column, with a description of the item and cost.

The following examples illustrate how the purchase journal and the accounts payable ledger work together. Star Company buys $3,500 worth of stars for resale. The stars are purchased from the following sources: $1,400 from Comet, $1,200 from

Asteroid, and $900 from Nebula. The purchases are made on credit. The completed Purchase Journal is shown below (see Figure 2-11).

Figure 2-11. Completed Purchase Journal

			Accounts Payable	Purchases	Supplies	Insurance		Amount
Date	Account Credited	Post	Credit	Debit	Debit	Debit	General	Debit
EOM	Comet Co.	AP C	_B_ **1,400**	1,400				
EOM	Asteroid Co.	AP A	_B_ **1,200**	1,200				
EOM	Nebula Co.	AP N	_B_ **900**	900				
	Total		**3,500**	**3,500**				
			GL7	GL 52				
			_A_	_C_				

PURCHASE JOURNAL — PJ 1

Note. The letters and numbers in italic type are explained below. Other postings and balances are also shown.

Posting A to General Ledger (GL 7)

From the total of the accounts payable column of the *purchase journal*, $3,500 is posted to the general ledger.

Purpose: to record the total amount of accounts payable for this accounting period into the general ledger.

ACCOUNTS PAYABLE (CONTROL)		GENERAL LEDGER				GL 7	
						Balance	
Date	Item	Post	Debit	Credit		Debit	Credit
EOM		PJ 1		_A_ **3,500**			

Posting <u>B</u> to Subsidiary Ledgers (AP C, AP A, and AP N)

The three intermediate items in the accounts payable column of the purchase journal $1,400, 1,200 and 900 (all *credits*) are posted as *credits* to their respective pages in the accounts payable ledger. Intermediate items are always of the same denomination as that of the column total; if the column total is a debit the intermediate items are debits, if the column total is a credit the intermediate items are credits.

ACCOUNTS PAYABLE LEDGER

					Balance	
Name: **COMET CO.**		*Terms:* Net 30				**AP C**
Date	*Item*	*Post*	*Debit*	*Credit*	*Debit*	*Credit*
EOM		PJ 1		***B 1,400***		
EOM		CD 1	***F 1,400***			

ACCOUNTS PAYABLE LEDGER

					Balance	
Name: **ASTEROID CO.**		*Terms:* 2% 10 Net 30				**AP A**
Date	*Item*	*Post*	*Debit*	*Credit*	*Debit*	*Credit*
EOM		PJ 1		***B 1,200***		

ACCOUNTS PAYABLE LEDGER

					Balance	
Name: **NEBULA CO.**		*Terms:* Net 60				**AP N**
Date	*Item*	*Post*	*Debit*	*Credit*	*Debit*	*Credit*
EOM		PJ 1		***B 900***		

Posting <u>C</u> to General Ledger (GL 52)

From the purchase column of the *purchase journal* the total, $3,500 (a *debit*), is posted as a *debit* to the *purchase* page of the *general ledger*, GL 52.

PURCHASES			GENERAL LEDGER			GL 52	
						Balance	
Date	Item	Post	Debit	Credit	Debit	Credit	
EOM		PJ 1	_C_ 3,500				

A column with the heading "accounts payable" in the check disbursement journal is always made by the bookkeeper when a business buys goods or services on credit. When a business purchases on credit it eventually pays by check. The following two postings (E and F) from the accounts payable column of the *check disbursement journal* illustrate how those payments are posted. The completed Check Disbursement Journal is shown below.

					CHECK DISBURSEMENT JOURNAL						CD 1	
JE No	Payee	Check No.	Bank Credit	Commission Debit	Tele-phone Debit	Rent Debit	Petty Cash Debit	Owner's Equity Debit	Accounts Payable Debit	Explanation	General Debit
3	Seaside Tel.	101	60		60						
5	Petty Cash	102	200				200				
6	Jo's Furniture	103	1,100							GL5 Equipment-F&F	1,100
7	Edgar Motors	104	1,500							GL5 Equipment-Truck	1,500
9	Alpine Bank	105	500							GL8 Loan Pay.able Alpine Bank	500
11	Fred Rentals	106	1,500			500				GL4 Deposit-Rent	1,000
12	John Roberts	107	450	CL R 450							
12	Robert Brown	108	600	CL B 600							
12	Stanley Steel	109	500	CL S 500							
13	Mr. Jones	110	800					800			
14	Comet Co.	111	1,400						_F 1,400_		
		Totals	8,610	1,550	60	500	200	800	_E 1,400_		4,100
			GL 1	GL 54	GL57	GL56	GL 2	GL 9	GL 7		

Posting E from the Check Disbursement Journal

From the *accounts payable* column of the *check disbursement journal* the total ($1,400, a *debit*) is posted as a *debit* to Accounts Payable account in the General Ledger. The *general ledger* (see Posting F below) is used to record the total. The subsidiary ledger is to record the 'who?' and the 'how much?'

Purpose: to record the reduction in the total amount of accounts payable during this accounting period.

ACCOUNTS PAYABLE (CONTROL)		GENERAL LEDGER				GL 7
					Balance	
Date	Item	Post	Debit	Credit	Debit	Credit
EOM		PJ 1		A 3,500		
EOM		CD 1	E 1,400			

Posting F from the Check Disbursement Ledger

The intermediate item of $1,400 is posted from the *accounts payable* column of the check disbursement journal to the Comet page in the Accounts Payable Ledger.

ACCOUNTS PAYABLE LEDGER					
Name: COMET COMPANY		Terms: NET 30			AP C
Date	Item	Post	Debit	Credit	Balance
EOM		PJ 1		C 1,400	
EOM		CD 1	F 1,400		

When the total, $1,400, of the accounts payable column of the check disbursement journal is posted to the general ledger (see Posting E), it is posted as a debit. When the intermediate item ($1,400) in the same column is posted to the accounts payable ledger, it is also posted as a debit.

In reality, the two $1,400 amounts are actually one amount, posted to two sets of books. The general ledger is one set of books (where the totals are kept) and the subsidiary ledgers are another set of books (which breaks down the total to its component parts).

By looking at GL 7 and AP C, above, a story is told, as follows: During the accounting period Star Company purchased $3,500 worth of merchandise, GL 7). Part of the total purchased, $1,400, was from comet (AP C). During the accounting period Star Company paid off a total of $1,400 to its creditors, GL7. One of the businesses which received payment was Comet (AP C).

Summary

All purchases made on credit are recorded in the *purchase journal*. The purchased item may be a component part of a manufactured product, an airplane ticket, outside labor, and so on. As long as it is to be paid for at some time in the future, it is recorded in the *purchase journal*. The additional columns in the purchase journal should have column headings to accommodate the most frequently used items and products purchased.

The total of the accounts payable column is posted to the accounts payable control page of the general ledger. The accounts payable control page of the general ledger, as the name implies, is in control of the accounts payable ledger. Any amount posted to the accounts payable control page of the general ledger must be posted to the accounts payable ledger, a subsidiary ledger. The accounts payable ledger contains individual pages for each creditor from which Star Company buys on credit.

11. The Sales Journal and Accounts Receivable Ledger

Sales made on credit are recorded, by invoice number, in the Sales Journal. Sales made on credit require the use of an Accounts Receivable Ledger, a subsidiary ledger, to keep records of who owes Star Company money.

For additional information regarding subsidiary ledgers refer to the Section 2, "Subsidiary Ledgers" in this Chapter.

The *sales journal* operates "hand-in-glove" with the *accounts receivable ledger*. The illustration below is typical of a sales journal page. There is one "sales" column shown in this Sales Journal. Some businesses might wish to break sales down into various categories, which would necessitate the use of two or more columns.

The purpose of the *general ledger* is to record the total amount due from creditors. The purpose of the *accounts receivable ledger* is to record the names and related details of each business that owe Star Company money.

For example, assume Star Company sells $7,500 worth of stars on credit, as follows: $2,400 to Venus, $2,500 to Mars, and $2,600 Pluto. This transaction is recorded in the sales journal below.

SALES JOURNAL						SJ 1
Date	Customer Charged	Invoice Number	Terms	Post to Acct. Rec. Ledger	Accounts Receivable Debit	Sales Post to GL51 Credit
EOM	Venus Co.	1108	2/10 N 30	AR V	*B* **2,400**	2,400
EOM	Mars Co.	1109	N 30	AR M	*B* **2,500**	2,500
EOM	Pluto Co.	1110	N 30	AR P	*B* **2,600**	2,600
	Totals				**7,500**	**7,500**
					GL3	GL51
					A	*C*

Note. The letters and numbers in italic type are explained below. Other postings and balances are also shown.

Posting *A* of the Sales Journal to General Ledger (GL 3)

The total of the *account receivable* column of the sales journal, $7,500, is posted to the *accounts receivable* control page of the general ledger, GL3. The *general ledger* keeps a record of the *total* amount due Star Company from all businesses that have made purchases on credit.

ACCOUNTS RECEIVABLE (CONTROL) GENERAL LEDGER					GL 3	
Date	Item	Post	Debit	Credit	Balance Debit	Credit
EOM		SJ1	*A* **7,500**			
EOM		CR1		*D* 1,500		

To keep a record of the "total" amount owed to Star Company is not adequate. It is necessary to know who owes the money, how much is owed and the terms of the sales. To accomplish this objective a subsidiary ledger called the Accounts Receivable Ledger is used.

Posting <u>B</u> of the Intermediate Amounts to Accounts Receivable Ledger

From the *accounts receivable* column of the sales journal, the intermediate amounts (highlighted in red) are posted to their respective pages in the *accounts receivable* ledger. The letters before the amounts indicate the page numbers to which the amounts are posted. The total of the accounts receivable column is posted, as always, to GL 3. Note that the amount posted to the general ledger is a debit and the amounts posted to the accounts receivable ledger is also a debit. Thus, the accounts receivable ledger retains the same denomination as its controlling account in the general ledger.

ACCOUNTS RECEIVABLE LEDGER					AR V
Name: **VENUS COMPANY**					
Date	*Terms*	*Post*	*Debit*	*Credit*	*Balance*
EOM	2/10 N30	SJ1	<u>*B*</u> *2,400*		

ACCOUNTS RECEIVABLE LEDGER					AR M
Name: **MARS COMPANY**					
Date	*Terms*	*Post*	*Debit*	*Credit*	*Balance*
EOM	N30	SJ1	<u>*B*</u> *2,500*		
EOM		CR1		<u>*D*</u> *1,500*	

ACCOUNTS RECEIVABLE LEDGER					AR P
Name: **PLUTO COMPANY**					
Date	*Terms*	*Post*	*Debit*	*Credit*	*Balance*
EOM	N30	SJ1	<u>*B*</u> *2,600*		

Posting C to General Ledger from Sales Journal

From the sales column of the *sales journal* the total amount of sales, $7,500, is posted to the sales page of the *general ledger, GL 51*. The posting of the sales journal is complete when the $7,500 in the sales column has been posted.

SALES			GENERAL LEDGER				GL 51
						Balance	
EOM	*Item*	*Post*	*Debit*	*Credit*		*Debit*	*Credit*
EOM		SJ 1		*C* 7,500			7,500

Payments received from customers. From time to time Star Company receives payments from customers that are posted to the *accounts receivable* column in the cash receipts journal (see below).

Posting D from Cash Receipts Journal to General Ledger Control Account

The Cash Receipts Journal reproduced below is to be used in connection with postings D and E. Posting D and E in the accounts receivable column demonstrates how payments are posted.

CASH RECEIPTS JOURNAL										CR 1
Date	*Account* *Credited*	Bank *Debit*	Cash *Sales* *Credit*	*Post*	**Accounts** **Receivable** *Credit*	*Post*	Loans *Payable* *Credit*	Owner's *Equity* *Credit*	*Explanation*	*General* *Credit*
EOM	Alpine Bank	5,000					5,000			
EOM	M. Jones	4,000						4,000		
EOM	Mars Co.	1,500		AR M	*E* 1,500					
	Totals	10,500			*D* 1,500		5,000	4,000		
					GL3					

From the accounts receivable column of the cash receipts journal the total ($1,500) is posted to the accounts receivable control page of the general ledger, page GL 3. This payment reduces the total amount of accounts receivable.

ACCOUNTS RECEIVABLE (CONTROL)		GENERAL LEDGER			GL 3	
					Balance	
Date	Item	Post	Debit	Credit	Debit	Credit
EOM		SJ 1	A 7,500			
EOM		CR 1		D 1,500		

Star Company's subsidiary ledgers are Accounts Receivable, Accounts Payable, and Commission. The posting to those ledgers are shown below.

Posting E to Subsidiary Ledger

From the accounts receivable column of the *cash receipts journal* the intermediate item $1,500 is posted to Mars Company in the *accounts receivable ledger*, page AR M.

ACCOUNTS RECEIVABLE LEDGER					AR M	
Name:	MARS COMPANY					
Date	Terms	Post	Debit	Credit	Balance	
EOM	N 30	SJ 1	B 2,500			
EOM		CR1		E 1,500		

12. The Commission Ledger

The management of Star Company decided that it would be desirable to have a *commission ledger* so that it would know at all times the amount of commission earned by each of the people who receive commission compensation. Very few businesses use *commission ledgers*.

The names and amounts of commission earned are recorded in the commission column of the *check disbursement journal*. The commission ledger contains individual pages on which to record the earnings of each of the payees.

The *commission ledger* created would be a subsidiary ledger because:

The total amount of commission is recorded on the commission page of the *general ledger* GL54.

The amount of commission earned by each individual is recorded on his or her page in the *commission ledger*.

The total of the commission page in the *general ledger* must be equal to the sum of the commission paid as shown in the commission ledger.

Depending on the desires of management, a subsidiary ledger can be made of many of the accounts listed on the chart of accounts. For example, a business might have many items or models and management might request of accounting that sales be broken-down as to item or model. If this would entail using too many columns in the sales journal a subsidiary ledger could be made for that purpose.

Note. Only the commission column of the check disbursement journal will be discussed in this section. The completed Check Disbursement Ledger follows:

CHECK DISBURSEMENT JOURNAL   *CD*   *1*

JE #	Payee	Chk No.	Bank Credit	Comm. Debit	Tele-phone Debit	Rent Debit	Petty Cash Debit	Owner's Equity Debit	Accounts Payable Debit	Explanation	General Debit
3	Seaside Tel.	101	60		60						
5	Petty Cash	102	200				200				
6	Jo's Furniture	103	1,100							GL5 Equipment - F&F	1,100
7	Edgar Motors	104	1,500							GL5 Equipment - Truck	1,500
9	Alpine Bank	105	500							GL8 Loan Pay. Alpine Bank	500
11	Fred Rentals	106	1,500			500				GL4 Deposit - Rent	1,000
12	John Roberts	107	450	*R CL R* 450							
12	Robert Brown	108	600	*B CL B* 600							
12	Stanley Steel	109	500	*S CL S* 500							
13	Mr. Jones	110	800					800			
14	Comet Co.	111	1,400						AP C 1,400		
		Total	8,610	*A* 1,550	60	500	200	800	1,400		4,100
			GL 1	**GL** 54	**GL** 57	**GL** 56	**GL** 2	**GL** 9	**GL** 7		

Note. The letters and numbers in italic type are explained below. Other postings and balances are also shown.

Posting *A* to General Ledger

From the total of the commission column in the check disbursement journal, $1,550 is posted to the commission page of the *general ledger*.

Account: **COMMISSION**		**GENERAL LEDGER**				**GL 54**
					Balance	
Date	Item	Post	Debit	Credit	Debit	Credit
EOM		CR 1	*A* *1,550*		1,550	

Reminder: The totals of columns with the headings accounts receivable, accounts Payable and Commission are posted to the general ledger and the intermediate items are posted to subsidiary ledgers.

Posting *R* to Subsidiary Ledger from Check Disbursement Journal

From the commission column of the *check disbursement journal*, $450 is posted to John Roberts's page of the *commission ledger*.

Name	**Roberts, John**	**COMMISSION LEDGER**				**CL R**
					Balance	
Date	Item	Post	Debit	Credit	Debit	Credit
EOM		CD 1	*R* *450*			

Posting *B* to Subsidiary Ledger from Check Disbursement Journal

From the commission column of the check *disbursement journal*, $600 is posted to Robert Brown's page of the commission ledger.

Name	**Brown, Robert**	**COMMISSION LEDGER**				**CL B**
					Balance	
Date	Item	Post	Debit	Credit	Debit	Credit
EOM		CD 1	*B* *600*			

Posting *S* to Subsidiary Ledger from Check Disbursement Journal

From the commission column of the *check disbursement journal*, $500 is posted to Stanley Steel's page of the *commission ledger*.

Name	Steel, Stanley		COMMISSION LEDGER			CL	S
						Balance	
Date	Item	Post	Debit	Credit	Debit	Credit	
EOM		CD 1	S 500				

Observations

➢ The commission ledger, accounts receivable ledger and the accounts payable ledger are subsidiary ledgers.

➢ The *accounts receivable ledger* and *accounts payable ledger* are used by businesses that use the accrual basis of accounting, explained in chapter 4.

➢ The *commission ledger* is used only when management wishes to accomplish a specific objective. Very few businesses use the commission ledger

➢ The total amount of commission paid is posted to the commission page of the *general ledger* (GL 54).

➢ All the recipients of commission are posted to their respective pages in the *commission ledger*.

➢ All postings to subsidiary ledgers are posted the same way as they appear in the *general ledger*. If the totals are debits in the *general ledger* they are debits in the subsidiary ledger. If the totals are credits in the *general ledger* they are credits in the subsidiary ledger.

➢ A summary of the postings (shown below) indicates where and how the commission column of *check disbursement ledger* (CDL) is posted.

From CDL	Amount:	Posted To:	Posted As:
The Total	$1,550	General Ledger	Debit
J. Roberts	450	Commission Ledger R	Debit
R. Brown	600	Commission Ledger B	Debit
S. Steel	500	Commission Ledger S	Debit

13. Establishing a Petty Cash Book

This section shows how to set-up a petty cash fund. This fund is used to reimburse people who have paid for minor items on behalf of the business. It explains how the petty cash fund is reimbursed and the journal entries and posting required.

Check number 102 was entered in the Cash Disbursement Journal and shows the issuance of the $200 check payable to Petty Cash. Only the petty cash column will be used in the following discussion.

CHECK DISBURSEMENT JOURNAL *CD 1*

JE No	Payee	Check No.	Bank Credit	Commiss. Debit	Tele-phone Debit	Rent Debit	**Petty Cash** Debit	Owner Equity Debit	Accounts Payable Debit	Explanation	General Debit
3	Seaside Tel.	101	60		60						
5	Petty Cash	102	200				200				
6	Jo's Furniture	103	1,100							GL5 Equipment-F&F	1,100
7	Edgar Motors	104	1,500							GL5 Equipment-Truck	1,500
9	Alpine Bank	105	500							GL8 Loan Pay. Alpine Bank	500
11	Fred Rentals	106	1,500			500				GL4 Deposit-Rent	1,000
12	John Roberts	107	450	CL R 450							
12	Robert Brown	108	600	CL B 600							
12	Stanley Steel	109	500	CL S 500							
13	Mr. Jones	110	800					800			
14	Comet Co.	111	1,400						AP C 1,400		
		Total	8,610	1,550	60	500	_A_ 200	800	1,400		4,100
			GL 1	GL 54	GL 57	GL 56	GL 2	GL 9	GL 7		

Item A. In order to set up a petty cash fund, check # 102, in the amount of $200, was issued from the check disbursement journal and is posted to the petty cash page of the general ledger. The petty cash page of the General Ledger (see below) reflects the posting of the $200 check.

PETTY CASH		GENERAL LEDGER				GL 2
					Balance	
Item	Post	Debit	Credit		Debit	Credit
	CD 1	_A_ 200			200	

Item B. When petty cash receives the $200 check it is cashed and the money is retained in the petty cash fund. With the passage of time the petty cash fund pays out $20 auto expense, $10 telephone, $160 food and lodging, for a total of $190. Vouchers and receipts were given by the recipients.

The vouchers, receipts, and a copy of the petty cash page are submitted to the accounting department together with a request for a $190 reimbursement check. The cashing of the check and the disbursement of $190 are posted to the petty cash book, as shown below.

PETTY CASH BOOK									PC 1
Date	Payee	Reimbursement Receipts Debit	Total Cash Distributed Credit	Auto	Telephone	Food and Lodging	Office Supplies	Postage	Explanation
EOM	Check 102	_B_ 200							
EOM	various		190	20	10	160			
	P C Balance	10							
	Check due	190							
	Balance	200							

Item C. In most cases a reimbursement check to petty cash would be issued, but the accounting department decides to show the amount due to petty cash by journal entry. Accounting makes journal entry 1A in the General Journal, see below.

GENERAL JOURNAL				GL 1	
Date		Post	Debit		Credit
EOM	**JE 1A**				
	Auto expense	GL 53	C	20	
	Telephone	GL 57	C	10	
	Food and Lodging	GL 55	C	160	
	Due petty cash	GL 2			C 190
	To record amount due petty cash				

And finally, journal entry **1A** of the general journal is posted to designated accounts in the general ledger.

AUTO EXPENSE		GENERAL LEDGER					GL 53
						Balance	
Date	Item	Post	Debit	Credit		Debit	Credit
EOM		JE 1A	C 20			20	

FOOD AND LODGING		GENERAL LEDGER					GL 55
						Balance	
Date	Item	Post	Debit	Credit		Debit	Credit
EOM		JE 1A	C 160			160	

TELEPHONE   **GENERAL LEDGER**   **GL 57**

					Balance	
Date	Item	Post	Debit	Credit	Debit	Credit
EOM		CD 1	60		60	
EOM		JE 1A	*C* *10*		70	

PETTY CASH   **GENERAL LEDGER**   **GL 2**

					Balance	
Date	Item	Post	Debit	Credit	Debit	Credit
EOM		CD 1	*A* *200*			
EOM		JE 1A		*C* *190*	10	

Chapter 3

Student Practice Session:

Posting From Journals to Ledgers

1. Introduction

All of the journals and ledgers previously explained are combined in this chapter. Each journal is displayed together with the general ledger and the subsidiary ledgers. The books to be studied include:

- Check Disbursement Journal
- Cash Receipts Journal
- Purchase Journal and Accounts Payable Ledger
- Sales journal and Accounts Receivable Ledger
- Posting to the General Ledger
- Posting to the Subsidiary Ledgers

2. Student Practice Sessions

A. The Check Disbursement Journal

What has been done

All the transactions pertaining to the check disbursement journal are enumerated below. The check disbursement journal has been totaled and cross-footed and is ready to be posted.

What is to be done by the student

1. Study the nine transactions below and see how they are recorded in the Check Disbursement Journal.

2. Refer to the Chart of Accounts (see Figure 3-1 below) and enter the General Ledger numbers under the column totals in the Check Disbursement Journal. For example, "Bank" is posted to GL 1.

3. Enter the posting *destination* of the intermediate items. When posting to the Accounts Payable Ledger use the symbol **AP** *plus* the first letter of the last name. For example, "AP C" stands for the *accounts payable* ledger page *C*, and represents the Comet Company in the subsidiary ledger.

4. After recording all the posting destinations in the Check Disbursement Journal, make the required postings to the General Ledgers and to the Subsidiary Ledgers. The General Ledger and Subsidiary Ledgers for this exercise are displayed beneath the Check Disbursement Journal.

5. When posting to ledgers, always enter the source number in the "post" column. In this exercise, the source is "CD 1," the Check Disbursement Journal, page 1.

Figure 3-1. Chart of Accounts Used in General Ledger

General Ledger Chart of Accounts	GL #
Balance Sheet Items	
Accounts Payable (Control)	7
Accounts Receivable (Control)	3
Bank	1
Deposits	4
Inventory	10
Loans Payable	8
Owner's Equity	9
Equipment	5
Petty Cash	2
Reserve for Depreciation	6
Profit and Loss Items	
Auto Expense	53
Commission (Control)	54
Food and Lodging	55
Depreciation	58
Profit & Loss	59
Purchases	52
Rent	56
Telephone	57
Sales	51

In the event of any difficulty, or to verify the accuracy of the postings, refer to Chapter 2. Complete postings of all the journals and ledgers are shown in Chapter 2.

The transactions affecting the Check Disbursement Journal are as follows:

Transaction #3

Star Company issues check #101 for $60 to Seaside Telephone for phone usage.

Transaction #5

Star Company issues check #102 for $200 in order to set up a petty cash fund to reimburse employees for cash expended on behalf of the company.

Transaction #6

Star Company issues check #103 in the amount of $1,100 to Jackson Furniture for the purchase of furniture and fixtures.

Transaction #7

Star Company gives check #104 for $1,500 to Edgar Motors to pay for a truck to be used in the business.

Transaction #9

Star Company issues check #105 in the amount of $500 to repay a portion of the $5,000 loan due to Alpine Bank.

Transaction #11

Star Company gives check #106 to Fern Rentals totaling $1,500. The check represents the payment of the current month's rent ($500), and a deposit of $1,000 for the last two months of a five-year lease.

Transaction #12

Star Company issues checks (#107, #108, and #109) for commissions as follows:

John Roberts - $450
Robert Brown - $600
Stanley Steel - $500

Transaction #13

Mr. Jones, owner of the business, requests funds for his own personal use from the bookkeeper. Star Company issues check #110 for $800 to Mr. Jones.

Transaction #14

Star Company issues check #111 for $1,400 to Comet Company, thereby reducing accounts payable.

The Check Disbursement Journal, showing the above transactions, is displayed below. The transaction numbers are indicated in the left column.

CHECK DISBURSEMENT JOURNAL CD 1

Trans. No	Payee	Check No.	Bank Credit	Commission Debit	Telephone Debit	Rent Debit	Petty Cash Debit	Owner's Equity Debit	Accounts Payable Debit	Explanation	General Debit
3	Seaside Telephone	101	60		60						
5	Petty Cash	102	200				200				
6	Jackson Furniture	103	1,000							Equipment F&F	1,100
7	Edgar Motors	104	1,500							Equipment Truck	1,500
9	Alpine Bank	105	500							Loan Payable Alpine Bank	500
11	Fern Rentals	106	1,500			500				Deposit Rent	1,000
12	John Roberts	107	450	450							
12	Robert Brown	108	600	650							
12	Stanley Steel	109	500	500							
13	Mr. Jones	110	800					800			
14	Comet Co	111	1,400						1,400		
		Totals:	8,610	1,550	60	500	200	800	1,400		4,100
			GL__	GL__	GL__	GL__	GL__	GL__	GL__		

Postings to the General Ledger–

BANK	GENERAL LEDGER					GL 1	
						Balance	
Date	Item	Post	Debit	Credit		Debit	Credit
EOM							

DEPOSITS	GENERAL LEDGER					GL 4	
						Balance	
Date	Item	Post	Debit	Credit		Debit	Credit
EOM	Rent-Fenway Rentals						

PETTY CASH   GENERAL LEDGER   GL 2

Date	Item	Post	Debit	Credit	Balance Debit	Credit
EOM						

EQUIPMENT   GENERAL LEDGER   GL 5

Date	Item	Post	Debit	Credit	Balance Debit	Credit
EOM	Furniture & Fixtures					
	Acq. 1/1/11, Life 8 years					
EOM	Truck, 2009 Rawley					
	Acq. 1/1/11, Life 5 yr.					

ACCOUNTS PAYABLE (CONTROL)   GENERAL LEDGER   GL 7

Date	Item	Post	Debit	Credit	Balance Debit	Credit
EOM						
EOM						

LOANS PAYABLE   GENERAL LEDGER   GL 8

Date	Item	Post	Debit	Credit	Balance Debit	Credit
EOM	Alpine Bank					

COMMISSION   GENERAL LEDGER   GL 54

Date	Item	Post	Debit	Credit	Balance Debit	Credit
EOM						

OWNER'S EQUITY		GENERAL LEDGER				GL 9
					Balance	
Date	Item	Post	Debit	Credit	Debit	Credit
EOM						

RENT		GENERAL LEDGER				GL 56
					Balance	
Date	Item	Post	Debit	Credit	Debit	Credit
EOM						

TELEPHONE		GENERAL LEDGER				GL 57
					Balance	
Date	Item	Post	Debit	Credit	Debit	Credit
EOM						

The subsidiary ledgers for this exercise are shown below.

Name	ROBERTS, JOHN	COMMISSION LEDGER				CL R
					Balance	
Date	Item	Post	Debit	Credit	Debit	Credit
EOM						

Name	STEEL, STANLEY	COMMISSION LEDGER				CL S
					Balance	
Date	Item	Post	Debit	Credit	Debit	Credit
EOM						

Name	BROWN, ROBERT	COMMISSION LEDGER				CL	B
						Balance	
Date	Item	Post	Debit	Credit	Debit	Credit
EOM						

ACCOUNTS PAYABLE LEDGER					AP C
Name: COMET COMPANY		Terms: NET 30			
Date	Item	Post	Debit	Credit	Balance
EOM					
EOM					

B. THE CASH RECEIPTS JOURNAL

What has been done

All the transactions have been entered into the Cash Receipts Journal. The cash receipts journal is totaled and cross-footed and is ready to be posted.

What is to be done by the student

1. Review the three transactions (1, 10, and 15) and study how they are recorded in the Cash Receipts Journal.

2. Refer to the Chart of Accounts (Figure 3-2 below) and enter the General Ledger numbers under the column totals in the Cash Receipts Journal. Also, record the posting destination of the intermediate items. When posting to the Accounts Receivable Ledger use the symbol **AR** *plus* the first letter of the last name.

3. After having recorded all the posting destinations, make the required postings to the General Ledgers and the Subsidiary Ledgers. The ledgers for this exercise are displayed beneath the cash receipts journal.

4. When posting to ledgers always enter the source number in the "post" column.

Figure 3-2. Chart of Accounts Used in General Ledger

General Ledger Chart of Accounts	GL #
Balance Sheet Items	
Accounts Payable (Control)	7
Accounts Receivable (Control)	3
Bank	1
Deposits	4
Inventory	10
Loans Payable	8
Owner's Equity	9
Equipment	5
Petty Cash	2
Reserve for Depreciation	6
Profit and Loss Items	
Auto Expense	53
Commission (Control)	54
Food and Lodging	55
Depreciation	58
Profit & Loss	59
Purchases	52
Rent	56
Telephone	57
Sales	51

In the event of any difficulty, or to verify the accuracy of the postings, refer to Chapter 2. Complete postings of all the journals and ledgers are shown in Chapter 2.

The transactions affecting bank deposits are as follows:

Transaction #1

Mr. Jones starts a new business, the Star Company, and he borrows $5,000 from the Alpine Bank, which he deposits into the business checking account.

Transaction #10

Mr. Jones withdraws $4,000 from his personal checking account and deposits the money into Star Company's checking account for business use.

Transaction #15

Star Company deposits a check for $1,500 from Mars reducing *accounts receivable.*

The Cash Receipts Journal, showing the above transactions, is displayed below.

				CASH RECEIPTS JOURNAL							CR 1
Date	Account Credited	Bank Debit	Cash Sales Credit	Post	Accounts Receivable Credit	Post	Loans Payable Credit	Owner's Equity Credit	Explanation		General Credit
EOM	Alpine Bank	5,000					5,000				
EOM	M. Jones	4,000						4,000			
EOM	Mars Co.	1,500			1,500						
	Totals:	10,500			1,500		5,000	4,000			

Postings to the General Ledger–

BANK		GENERAL LEDGER				GL 1	
						Balance	
Date	Item	Post	Debit	Credit		Debit	Credit
EOM							

ACCOUNTS RECEIVABLE (CONTROL)		GENERAL LEDGER				GL 3
					Balance	
Date	Item	Post	Debit	Credit	Debit	Credit
EOM						

Helpful Tip. All total amounts posted to the accounts receivable (control) page of the general ledger GL 3 above) must equal the intermediate item or items that make up that total posted to the accounts receivable subsidiary ledger (AR M below).

LOANS PAYABLE		GENERAL LEDGER				GL 8
					Balance	
Date	Item	Post	Debit	Credit	Debit	Credit
EOM						

OWNER'S EQUITY		GENERAL				GL 9
					Balance	
Date	Item	Post	Debit	Credit	Debit	Credit
EOM						

Posting to the Accounts Receivable Subsidiary Ledger–

ACCOUNTS RECEIVABLE LEDGER					AR M
Name: **MARS COMPANY**					
Date	Terms	Post	Debit	Credit	Balance
EOM	N30				
EOM					

C. THE PURCHASE JOURNAL

What has been done

Transaction #2 has been entered into the Purchase Journal. The Purchase Journal is totaled and cross-footed and is ready to be posted.

What is to be done by the student

1. Review the transaction (#2 below) and study how it is recorded in the Purchase Journal.

2. Refer to the Chart of Accounts (Figure 3-3 below) and enter the General Ledger number under the column totals in the Purchase Journal. Also, enter the posting destination of the intermediate items. When posting to the Accounts Payable ledger use symbol AP plus the first letter of the last name.

3. After having recorded all the posting destinations, make the required posting to the General Ledgers and the Subsidiary Ledgers. The ledgers for this exercise are displayed beneath the Purchase Journal.

Figure 3-3. Chart of Accounts Used in General Ledger

General Ledger Chart of Accounts	GL #
Balance Sheet Items	
Accounts Payable (Control)	7
Accounts Receivable (Control)	3
Bank	1
Deposits	4
Inventory	10
Loans Payable	8
Owner's Equity	9
Equipment	5
Petty Cash	2
Reserve for Depreciation	6
Profit and Loss Items	
Auto Expense	53
Commission (Control)	54
Food and Lodging	55
Depreciation	58
Profit & Loss	59
Purchases	52
Rent	56
Telephone	57
Sales	51

In the event of any difficulty, or to verify the accuracy of the postings, refer to Chapter 2. Complete postings of all the journals and ledgers are shown in Chapter 2.

The transactions affecting Purchases and Accounts Payable are as follows:

Transaction #2

Star Company buys $3,500 of stars for resale. The stars are purchased from the following sources: $1,400 from Comet, $1,200 from Asteroid, and $900 from Nebula.

The Purchase Journal, showing the above transaction, is displayed below.

PURCHASE JOURNAL								PJ 1
Date	Account Credited	Post	Accounts Payable Credit	PURCHASES Debit	Supplies Debit	Insurance Debit	General	Amount Debit
EOM	Comet Co.		1,400	1,400				
EOM	Asteroid Co.		1,200	1200				
EOM	Nebula Co.		900	900				
	Total		3,500	3,500				

Postings to the General Ledger–

ACCOUNTS PAYABLE (CONTROL)		GENERAL LEDGER				GL 7	
Date	Item	Post	Debit	Credit	Balance Debit	Credit
EOM						

PURCHASES		GENERAL LEDGER				GL 52	
Date	Item	Post	Debit	Credit	Balance Debit	Credit
EOM						

The subsidiary ledgers for this exercise are shown below.

ACCOUNTS PAYABLE LEDGER

Name:	**COMET CO.**		Terms:	NET 30		**AP C**
Date	Item	Post	Debit	Credit	Balance
EOM					

ACCOUNTS PAYABLE LEDGER

Name:	**ASTEROID CO.**		Terms:	2% 10 NET 30		**AP A**
Date	Item	Post	Debit	Credit	Balance
EOM					

ACCOUNTS PAYABLE LEDGER

Name	**NEBULA CO.**		Terms:	2% 10 NET 30		**AP N**
Date	Item	Post	Debit	Credit	Balance
EOM					

D. THE SALES JOURNAL

What has been done

All transactions have been entered into the Sales Journal. The Sales Journal has been totaled and cross-footed and is ready to be posted.

What is to be done by the student

1. Review transaction (#4 below) and observe how it is recorded in the Sales Journal.

2. Refer to the Chart of Accounts (see Figure 3-4) and enter the General Ledger numbers under the column totals.

3. Record the posting destination of the intermediate items. When posting to the Accounts Receivable Ledger use symbol **AR** *plus* first letter of the last name.

4. After recording all the posting destinations, post to the General Ledger and the Subsidiary Ledger. The ledgers for this exercise are beneath the Sales Journal.

Figure 3-4. Chart of Accounts Used in General Ledger

General Ledger Chart of Accounts	GL #
Balance Sheet Items	
Accounts Payable (Control)	7
Accounts Receivable (Control)	3
Bank	1
Deposits	4
Inventory	10
Loans Payable	8
Owner's Equity	9
Equipment	5
Petty Cash	2
Reserve for Depreciation	6
Profit and Loss Items	
Auto Expense	53
Food and Lodging	55
Depreciation	58
Profit & Loss	59
Purchases	52
Rent	56
Telephone	57
Sales	51

In the event of any difficulty, or to verify the accuracy of the postings, refer to Chapter 2. Complete postings of all the journals and ledgers are shown in Chapter 2.

The only transaction that affected the Sales Journal is as follows:

Transaction #4

Star Company sells $7,500 worth of stars on credit, as follows: $2,400 to Venus, $2,500 to Mars, and $2,600 Pluto.

The Sales Journal, showing the above transaction, follows:

					Accounts Receivable	Sales
	SALES JOURNAL					SJ 1
Date	Customer Charged	Invoice Number	Terms	Post to Acct. Rec. Ledger	Post to GL3 Debit	Post to GL51 Credit
JE 4	Venus Co.	1108	2 /10/ N 30		2,400	2,400
JE 4	Mars Co.	1109	N 30		2,500	2,500
JE 4	Pluto Co.	1110	N 30		2,600	2,600
	Total				7,500	7,500

Postings to the General Ledger–

ACCOUNTS RECEIVABLE	GENERAL LEDGER					GL 3
					Balance	
Date	Item	Post	Debit	Credit	Debit	Credit
EOM						

SALES	GENERAL LEDGER					GL 51
					Balance	
Date	Item	Post	Debit	Credit	Debit	Credit
EOM						

Posting to the Accounts Receivable Subsidiary Ledgers–

ACCOUNTS RECEIVABLE LEDGER					AR V
Name: **VENUS COMPANY**					
Date	Terms	Post	Debit	Credit	Balance
EOM	2/10 N30				

ACCOUNTS RECEIVABLE LEDGER					AR M
Name: **MARS COMPANY**					
Date	Terms	Post	Debit	Credit	Balance
EOM	N30				

ACCOUNTS RECEIVABLE LEDGER					AR P
Name: **PLUTO COMPANY**					
Date	Terms	Post	Debit	Credit	Balance
EOM	N30				

Chapter 4

Combining the Books and Preparing Financial Statements

1. Introduction

The journals prepared in Chapter 2 will be used to create a General Ledger in Chapter 4. The numbers contained in the General Ledger are used to make the Trial Balance. After the adjusting entries are made to the Trial Balance, the Balance Sheet and Profit and Loss Statement can be prepared. See Exhibit 4-1 at the end of this chapter.

In this chapter the following will be displayed and explained:

- A General ledger that was produced as the books were being assembled in Chapter 2
- The posting from the General Ledger to the Trial Balance
- The adjusting and closing entries
- The Balance Sheet and the Profit and Loss
- Explanations of the accrual basis and cash basis systems of accounting.

2. THE STAR COMPANY GENERAL LEDGER

In Chapter 2, each of the journals was explained. With each explanation, the page or pages of the general ledger used in the explanation was displayed. All the general ledger pages used in the explanations appear below.

All data recorded in the accounting books ultimately end up as debits or credits in the *general ledger*. At the end of each accounting period the debits and credits in the *general ledger* are netted out and the net amount is shown as a debit or credit in the "balance" column of the *general ledger*. Later, when the bookkeeper prepares the Trial Balance the net amount is recorded onto the *trial balance*. See Appendix B, *General Ledger Flow Chart*.

There are 19 accounts in the Star Company general ledger. All the accounts having an amount in the "balance column" of the general ledger are posted to the trial balance.

For example, in the general ledger, page 1, shown below, the amount $10,500 was posted from page 1 of the cash receipts journal and $8,610 was posted from page 1 of the *check disbursement journal*. The net amount $1,890 ($10,500 - $8,600), which is recorded in the balance column, is then posted to the trial balance.

BANK **GENERAL LEDGER** **GL 1**

Date	Item	Post	Debit	Credit	Balance Debit	Balance Credit
EOM		CD 1		8,610		
EOM		CR 1	10,500		1,890	

PETTY CASH **GENERAL LEDGER** **GL 2**

Date	Item	Post	Debit	Credit	Balance Debit	Balance Credit
EOM		CD 1	200			
EOM		JE 1A		190	10	

ACCOUNTS RECEIVABLE (CONTROL) **GENERAL LEDGER** **GL 3**

Date	Item	Post	Debit	Credit	Balance Debit	Balance Credit
EOM		CR 1		1,500		
EOM		SJ 1	7,500			
EOM		J 1		100	5,900	

DEPOSITS **GENERAL LEDGER** **GL 4**

Date	Item	Post	Debit	Credit	Balance Debit	Balance Credit
EOM	Rent-Fenway Rentals	CD 1	1,000		1,000	

EQUIPMENT — GENERAL LEDGER — GL 5

Date	Item	Post	Debit	Credit	Balance Debit	Balance Credit
EOM	Furniture & Fixtures Acq. 1/1/11 Life 8 years	CD 1	1,100			
EOM	Truck, 2009 Rawley Acq. 1/1/11 Life 5 years	CD 1	1,500		2,600	

RESERVE FOR DEPRECIATION — GENERAL LEDGER — GL 6

Date	Item	Post	Debit	Credit	Balance Debit	Balance Credit
EOM	Furniture and Fixtures	JE 2		138		
EOM	Truck	JE 2		300		438

ACCOUNTS PAYABLE (CONTROL) — GENERAL LEDGER — GL 7

Date	Item	Post	Debit	Credit	Balance Debit	Balance Credit
EOM		CD 1	1,400			
EOM		PJ 1		3,500		2,100

LOANS PAYABLE — GENERAL LEDGER — GL 8

Date	Item	Post	Debit	Credit	Balance Debit	Balance Credit
EOM	Alpine Bank	CR 1		5,000		
EOM	Alpine Bank	CD 1	500			4,500

OWNER'S EQUITY — GENERAL LEDGER — GL 9

Date	Item	Post	Debit	Credit	Balance Debit	Balance Credit
EOM		CR 1		4,000		
EOM		CD 1	800			
EOM		JE 4		1,562		4,762

INVENTORY — GENERAL LEDGER — GL 10

Date	Item	Post	Debit	Credit	Balance Debit	Balance Credit
EOM		JE 3	400		400	

SALES — GENERAL LEDGER — GL 51

EOM	Item	Post	Debit	Credit	Balance Debit	Balance Credit
EOM		SJ 1		7,500		
EOM		J 1	100			7,400

PURCHASES — GENERAL LEDGER — GL 52

Date	Item	Post	Debit	Credit	Balance Debit	Balance Credit
EOM		PJ 1	3,500			
EOM		J 3		400	3,100	

AUTO EXPENSE — GENERAL LEDGER — GL 53

Date	Item	Post	Debit	Credit	Balance Debit	Balance Credit
EOM		PC 1	20		20	

COMMISSION CONTROL)   **GENERAL LEDGER**   **GL 54**

Date	Item	Post	Debit	Credit	Balance Debit	Balance Credit
EOM		CR 1	1,550		1,550	

FOOD AND LODGING   **GENERAL LEDGER**   **GL 55**

Date	Item	Post	Debit	Credit	Balance Debit	Balance Credit
EOM		PC 1	160		160	

RENT   **GENERAL LEDGER**   **GL 56**

Date	Item	Post	Debit	Credit	Balance Debit	Balance Credit
EOM		CR 1	500		500	

TELEPHONE   **GENERAL LEDGER**   **GL 57**

Date	Item	Post	Debit	Credit	Balance Debit	Balance Credit
EOM		CD 1	60			
EOM		PC 1	10		70	

DEPRECIATION   **GENERAL LEDGER**   **GL 58**

Date	Item	Post	Debit	Credit	Balance Debit	Balance Credit
EOM		JE 2	438		438	

PROFIT AND LOSS   **GENERAL LEDGER**   **GL 59**

Date	Item	Post	Debit	Credit	Balance Debit	Balance Credit
EOM		JE 4	1,562		1,562	

The general ledger pages, shown above, contain all the postings of Star Company's journals to the general ledger. The total of each account is netted so that only the net amount appears in the balance column of the general ledger.

3. Preparing the Trial Balance

After all transactions have been recorded and posted into the *general ledger*, the bookkeepers prepare the *trial balance* using the net amount that appears in the balance column of each *general ledger* page. In preparing the trial balance, as each page of the general ledger is turned over, the amount in the balance column is noted on the trial balance as shown below.

A trial balance can be prepared at the end of the month to prove the general ledger is accurate. The trial balance is in "balance" when the totals of the debit and credit columns are in agreement.

Note. The fact the trial balance is in balance does not necessarily mean an error has not occurred. For example if an item that should have been posted to "rent" was erroneously posted to "equipment" the trial balance would be in balance, but an error has occurred.

At this point, the amounts recorded in the balance column of the general ledger are entered onto the trial balance. After the trial balance is added and it is ascertained it is mathematically correct, the adjusting entries are posted.

After all the required postings are made to the general ledger, the total of each account is netted so that only one number appears in the balance column of the ledger. Below is the end-of-month Trial Balance of Star Company.

The end-of-period Trial Balance of the Star Company follows.

Star Company Trial Balance EOM		
	Balance Sheet Items	
	Debit	*Credit*
Bank	1,890	
Petty Cash	10	
Accounts Receivable	5,900	
Deposit-Rent	1,000	
Equipment	2,600	
Depreciation Reserve		
Accounts Payable		2,100
Inventory		
Loans Payable		4,500
Owner's Equity		3,200
Total Balance Sheet Items:	**11,400**	**9,800**
	Profit & Loss Items	
Sales		
Purchases	3,500	
Depreciation		
Auto Expense	20	
Telephone	70	
Commission	1,550	
Food and Lodging	160	
Rent	500	
Profit		
Total Profit and Loss items:	**5,800**	**7,400**
Trial Balance Total:	**17,200**	**17,200**

4. Adjusting Entries

The adjusting and closing entries to be used in Star Company income tax return and other permanent documents are recorded in the *general journal* and posted. However, if an *interim* report is being prepared, the journal entries are recorded on work sheets rather than the general journal, and the books of account continue on as if no financial statement had been made. Journal entries may be made at any time in the general journal in order to rectify an error in the books of account or to record an unusual transaction, and so on. Adjusting entries typically are made at the end of an accounting period. Generally, a monthly, quarterly, or a yearly accounting period is used. The adjusting entries have already been posted into the adjusting entry column of the financial statement.

The general journal adjusting entries, shown below, pertain to the Star Company and are for informative purposes. There are many other adjusting entries that can be made. For example, when a business has prepaid its insurance premium, the portion used during the accounting period can be expensed. If a business owes money for a mortgage on a building it owns, the consumed portion of the interest can be expensed. In both cases, the unused portion remains on the balance sheet. When the accountant makes adjusting entries, work sheets are used to back up the entries.

The next step in the process is for the accountant to record the adjusting entries into the general journal. In the section, below, preceding the display of the actual general journal a more complete explanation of each journal entry is given.

Adjusting Entry	Explanation
JE 2	*To record depreciation of assets over useful life.* Straight line depreciation is used. It is assumed the furniture and fixtures will last 8 years and the truck 5 years. Thus, $138 ($1,100 ÷ 8) is expensed for the depreciation of the furniture and fixtures and $300 ($1,500 ÷ 5 (assumed useful life)) is depreciated for the truck. [See Note following Journal Entry 6 in Chapter 1.]
JE 3	*To record inventory.* Inventory is the value of merchandise available for sale at the end of the accounting period as compared to the merchandise available at the beginning of the accounting period. Star Company had no inventory at the beginning of the accounting period, but did have a $400 inventory at the end of the accounting period. The fluctuations in inventory for each accounting period are recorded by debiting or crediting purchases. In this case, inventory was added, thus the change was a *credit* to Purchases (affecting profit and loss). A debit is made to Inventory (a balance sheet item).
JE 4	*To transfer profits.* To close-out (transfer) profit and loss accounts to the Owner's Equity. Because there was a profit, *profit & loss* is debited, and *owner's equity* is credited
Closing Entry	*To close out profit and loss accounts.* A journal entry is prepared at the end of the accounting period to eliminate (zero out) the balances in Profit & Loss. As a result of this entry, the affected account will show $0 as a beginning balance at the start of the next accounting cycle.

Star Company is preparing a year end financial statement, which means the adjusting entries are made in the general journal. If this was an interim report the adjusting entries would be made on worksheets. An illustration of the General Journal showing the Adjusting Entries and Closing Entries follow.

Date	GENERAL JOURNAL	Post	Debit	GJ 1 Credit
	Adjusting Entries			
EOM	**JE 2**			
	Depreciation	GL 58	438	
	Reserve for depreciation—F & F	GL 6		138
	Reserve for depreciation—Truck	GL 6		300
	To record depreciation.			
EOM	**JE 3**			
	Inventory	GL 10	400	
	Purchases	GL 52		400
	To record inventory.			
EOM	**JE 4**			
	Profit	GL 59	1,562	
	Owner's Equity	GL 9		1,562
	To transfer profit.			
	Closing Entry			
	Sales	GL 51	7,400	
	Purchases	GL 52		3,100
	Auto expense	GL 53		20
	Commission	GL 54		1,550
	Food and Lodging	GL 55		160
	Rent	GL 56		500
	Telephone	GL 57		70
	Depreciation	GL 58		438
	Profit	GL 59		1,562
	To close out profit and loss accounts.			

After the trial balance is added and it is ascertained it is mathematically correct, the trial balance and the adjusting entries are combined as shown below. In the following illustration, the adjusting entries are entered in the two columns following the trial balance.

Star Company Adjusted Trial Balance
For Period Ended EOM

	Trial Balance Balance Sheet Items		Adjusting Entries		Balance Sheet	
	Debit	Credit	Debit	Credit	Debit	Credit
Bank	1,890				1,890	
Petty Cash	10				10	
Accounts Receivable	5,900				5,900	
Deposit-Rent	1,000				1,000	
Equipment	2,600				2,600	
Depreciation Reserve				JE 2 438		438
Accounts Payable		2,100				2,100
Inventory			JE 3 400		400	
Loans Payable		4,500				4,500
Owner's Equity		3,200		JE 4 1,562		4,762
Total:	**11,400**	**9,800**			**11,800**	**11,800**
	Profit & Loss Items				**Profit & Loss**	
Sales						7,400
Purchases	3,500			JE 3 400	3,100	
Depreciation			JE 2 438		438	
Auto Expense	20				20	
Telephone	70				70	
Commission	1,550				1,550	
Food and Lodging	160				160	
Rent	500				500	
Profit			JE 4 1,562		1,562	
Total:	**5,800**	**7,400**	**2,438**	**2,438**	**7,400**	**7,400**
Trial Balance Total:	**17,200**	**17,200**				

Finally, the adjusting entries are posted to the trial balance and the Balance Sheet and the Profit and Loss statement are created. When separated, the Balance Sheet and Profit and Loss Statement would be more formally displayed as shown below.

The Star Company EOM	BALANCE SHEET	
	Debit	Credit
Bank	1,890	
Petty Cash	10	
Accounts Receivable	5,900	
Deposit-Rent	1,000	
Equipment	2,600	
Depreciation Reserve		438
Accounts Payable		2,100
Inventory	400	
Loans Payable		4,500
Owner's Equity		4,762
Total:	11,800	11,800

The Star Company EOM	PROFIT & LOSS	
	Debit	Credit
Sales		7,400
Purchases	3,100	
Depreciation	438	
Auto Expense	20	
Telephone	70	
Commission	1,550	
Food and Lodging	160	
Rent	500	
Profit for Period:	1,562	
Total:	7,400	7,400

5. Accrual Basis of Accounting

The accrual basis of accounting assumes that income is recognized in the current accounting period when *earned* and *not* when *received*. Expenses are recognized when incurred, not when paid for. Accrual entries are made in order to record unrecorded revenue and unrecorded expenses. Most businesses use the accrual method of accounting.

Assume the monthly rent of $500 that was due on December 31, was not paid. The adjusting accrual entry to record the unpaid rent would be:

	Debit	*Credit*
Rent (profit and loss item)	500	
Rent Payable (balance sheet item)		500

The affect of the above journal entry is the expense is taken in the current year. The $500 expense is recorded in the profit and loss section. Rent payable would be a balance sheet item, which would increase the liability portion of the balance sheet by $500. This, of course, would reduce net worth by a like amount. The following year, when the rent was actually paid, the journal entry to record the payment of rent would be:

	Debit	*Credit*
Rent Payable (balance sheet item)	500	
Bank (balance sheet item)		500

Note. The net result of these entries was to put the expense in the year it was incurred and not in the year it was paid.

When an accrual type adjusting entry is made, one part of the journal entry is posted to profit and loss and the other part of the entry is posted to the balance sheet. There is no rent payable page in the general ledger. It is incumbent on the bookkeeper or accountant to make a page in the general ledger for this purpose even if the page is made December 31st and zeroed out January 1st.

6. Prepaid Expense Account

Some businesses use a prepaid expense asset account (balance sheet item) into which all the expenses that are paid for in advance are recorded. For example, if the yearly cost for maintenance is $1,200 and a check is issued July 1, the prepaid expenditure would be recorded into the prepaid expense account. In each of the succeeding months maintenance would be debited for $100 and the prepaid expense asset account would be credited until such time as it is depleted.

7. Cash Basis of Accounting

The cash basis of accounting recognizes revenue and expenses only when cash is received or expended. When a sale is made on credit during one accounting period, the amount of the sale is not included in the sales figure for that accounting period unless it was paid for during that same accounting period. The same holds true for purchases. In the cash basis system, *accounts receivable* and *accounts payable* ledgers are not used and purchases and sales are not recognized until such time as they are paid for. The cash basis system is mainly used by individuals for income tax purposes. Most businesses use the accrual basis of accounting.

8. Deferrals

Deferrals entries are made to adjust the amounts of expenses and revenue previously recorded during the current accounting period. When the amounts of expense or revenue includes a portion that is payable or receivable in the next accounting period, a deferral adjusting entry should be made. For example, assume an annual calendar year accounting period and a $1,200 payment for a new insurance policy is made on July 1. The insurance coverage period is July 1, in the current accounting cycle, through June 30 of the following year. The entry that should be made to reflect the 6 months of insurance expense during the current accounting period is as follows:

	Debit	*Credit*
Prepaid Insurance	600	
Insurance		600

9. Interim Financial Statements

Interim financial statements are those statements prepared for a period shorter than a calendar or a fiscal year. These statements could be monthly, quarterly or for any period of time, excluding year end.

When the accountant is asked to prepare interim financial statements the procedure is somewhat different from the preparation of a year-end financial statement. The trial balance is prepared in the same manner it usually is. Generally accepted accounting principles require that adjustments be made to reflect profit and loss correctly. However, in making interim statements, it is not necessary to record the adjusting entries in the *general journal* or to post the entries to any other journal or ledger. The accountant records the adjusting entries on a worksheet. After the trial balance has been entered, all the work is done on worksheets.

In making interim financial statements, the information contained in the General Ledger is used to make a trial balance. And that's all. The books of account remain the same as they were prior to making the interim statement. Thus, when bookkeeping resumes, the books are continued just as they were before the interim statements were prepared.

A. Balance Sheet

The balance sheet reflects everything that has happened within a business since inception. The balance sheet is a detailed presentation of all the assets and all the liabilities of a business at a specific moment in time. It indicates to viewers the financial strength of a business. It is an equation where the assets minus the liabilities equal the book value of a business.

Assets minus **Liabilities** = **Owner's Equity** (net worth of business)

B. Income Statement

The income statement is a financial report that exhibits income, expenses and the net income or net loss for a period of time. The report lists the income and expenses. A comparison of the two lists will show either the net income or the net loss. When total income exceeds total expenses, the excess is the net income for the period. When total expenses exceed total income the excess is net loss for the period.

The Star Company
Income Statement
EOM

Income:		
Sales		$7,400
Expenses:		
Purchases	$3,100	
Depreciation	438	
Auto Expense	20	
Telephone	70	
Commission	1,550	
Food and Lodging	160	
Rent	500	− 5,838
Net Profit:	$5,838	$1,562

Basic Accounting Simplified

Appendices

Appendix A

Glossary of Terms

Accounting

Accounting is the basis for recording transactions, maintaining financial records, performing internal audits, reporting and analyzing financial information to management, and giving advice on tax matters. It is a systematic process whereby business transactions are recorded in order to clarify financial information. *Accounting* reveals income for a given period, imparts information as to value and type of a firm's assets, liabilities, and owners' equity.

Accounting Period

An *accounting period* is a period of time (generally a period of one month or three months), but no more than a year, covered by financial statements.

Accounts Payable Control Account

The *accounts payable control account* is a specific page in the general ledger which is equal to the sum of the balances in the accounts payable ledger.

Accounts Payable Ledger

The *accounts payable ledger* keeps a record of the amount owed by the business. The accounts payable ledger, a subsidiary, keeps a record of all creditors from which a business has made purchases on credit. It has a different page for each creditor. The pages contain the name and address of the creditor, the date of purchases, the amount and terms, and payments made to the creditor. The sum of all the pages in the accounts payable ledger is equal to the accounts payable control page of the general ledger.

Accounts Receivable Control Account

The *accounts payable control account* is a specific page in the general ledger, which is equal to the sum of the balances in the accounts receivable ledger.

Accounts Receivable Ledger

The *accounts receivable ledger,* a subsidiary ledger, keeps a record of the amount owed to the business by creditors. The sum of all the pages in the *accounts receivable ledger* is equal to the accounts receivable control page of the general ledger.

Accrual Basis of Accounting

The *accrual basis of accounting* assumes that income is recognized when earned and not when received. Expenses are recognized when incurred, not when paid for. Accrual entries are made in order to show unrecorded revenue and unrecorded expenses. Most businesses use the accrual method of accounting.

Adjusting Entries

Adjusting entries are posted at the end of an accounting period and are used to assign expenses to the period in which they were incurred, and revenue to the period in which it was earned. [Compare to "Closing Entries."]

Assets

Assets are all the items in the possession of a business that are good for the business. Having more money in the bank, large accounts receivable, more inventory, more equipment, and so on, are examples of assets.

Balance Sheet

The *balance sheet* is a detailed presentation of all the assets and all the liabilities of a business at a specific moment in time. The *balance sheet* is an indication of the financial strength of a business at that time. The total value of the business assets must be equal to total value of the business liabilities plus the owner's equity. The *balance sheet* reflects everything that has happened within a business since inception.

Bank Statement

A record sent by the bank to a business usually on a monthly basis. It indicates all the activities within the account during the record period. Such activities may include: checks paid, deposits, withdrawals, and other transfers.

Bookkeeping

Bookkeeping is the process of recording financial transactions and keeping financial records.

Book Value

The value of a business as reflected in the books without taking into consideration the increase or decrease in fair market value is called *book value*.

Business

Business is a financial process within an organization in which goods and services are sold or exchanged, on the basis of their perceived worth. A business requires some type of investment and an adequate number of customers to whom its product can be sold at profit on a consistent basis. The owners and operators of a private, for-profit business have as one of their main objectives the receipt (or generation) of a financial return in exchange for work and acceptance of risk. A business can also be formed as a not-for-profit organization or be state-owned.

Cash Basis of Accounting

The cash basis of accounting recognizes revenue and expenses only when cash is received or expended. When a sale is made on credit during one accounting period the amount of the sale is not included in the sales figure for that accounting period unless it was paid for during the same accounting period. The same holds true for purchases. In the cash basis accounts receivable and accounts payable ledgers are not used and purchases and sales are not recognized until such time as they are paid for. The cash basis system is mainly used by individuals for income tax purposes.

Chart of Accounts

The chart of accounts serves the same function in accounting as the table of contents found at the beginning of a book. The chart, provided by the accountant, advises the bookkeeper with the means of determining the accounts included in the general ledger and their page numbers within the general ledger.

Check Disbursement Journal

All businesses issue checks to pay for goods and services purchased. At some point, these checks are recorded in the *check disbursement journal* as part of the accounting process.

In the *check disbursement journal*, the first column with the heading "Bank" is the master column. The amount of the check listed under that column is extended to the column whose heading best describes the purpose for which it was issued.

Closing Entries

Closing entries are the final bookkeeping entries made at the end of an accounting period to reduce all temporary accounts in the profit and loss to zero.

Control Account

A control account is a one-page summary account in the general ledger. The details that support the balance in the summary account are contained in a subsidiary ledger—a ledger outside of the general ledger. The purpose of the control account is to keep the general ledger to a manageable size by keeping details of transaction (needed by management) in a subsidiary ledger.

Cross Foot

To verify the sum of the totals in all the other columns agrees to the total of the master column.

Deferral Entry

A *deferral entry* is a journal entry made to adjust the amounts of expenses and revenue previously recorded during the current accounting period.

Deposit-In-Transit

A deposit-in-transit is a recent bank deposit that has not been recorded on the bank statement.

Depreciate or Depreciation

To "depreciate" an item means to write-off (expense) the value of an asset over its useful life.

Depreciation–Straight Line Method

The total cost of a depreciable asset, less any residual value, is written off over the life of the asset.

Fixed Assets

An asset having a useful life of one-year or more is called a *fixed asset*.

General Journal

A common type of journal used in keeping a chronological record of financial transactions of a business not belonging to other "special" journals (e.g., Sales Journal), or where no special journal exists. Thus, a *general journal* is used when it is necessary to record transactions that can't be conveniently recorded elsewhere.

General Ledger

The *general ledger* is the central repository of all the accounting information in which the summaries of all financial transactions (culled from subsidiary ledgers) during an accounting period are recorded. The general ledger contains the totals of all the items posted to subsidiary ledgers.

The *general ledger* is also called "the book of final entry," because it provides the entire data for preparing the financial statement of the business (or organization).

Income Statement

The income statement is a financial report that exhibits income, expenses, and the net income or net loss for a period of time.

Interim Financial Statements

Interim financial statements arc those statements prepared for a period shorter than a calendar or a fiscal year. These statements could be monthly, quarterly or for any period of time, excluding year end. Interim statements are different from the preparation of a year-end statement. In making interim statements it is not necessary to record the adjusting entries in the general journal or to post the entries to any other journal or ledger. The accountant records the adjusting entries on a worksheet. After the trial balance has been entered, all work is done on worksheets.

"Intermediate Items"

The term *intermediate items*, as used in this book, are all the items between the column heading and the column total that are located in journal columns with the headings Accounts Payable, Accounts Receivable, and Commission. Intermediate items are always posted to subsidiary ledgers.

Inventory

The value of saleable merchandise on hand at the end of an accounting period.

Journal

A *journal* is a book of original or first entry. The information gathered by the journals is posted into ledgers. For example, the Purchase Journal records, on a daily basis, all the purchases that are made on credit. And the Sales Journal records all the sales made on credit in a like manner.

Journal Entry

A *journal entry* is a logging of transactions into accounting journal items. That recordation is called a journal entry. The journal entry can consist of several items, each of which is either a debit or a credit. The total of the debits must equal the total of the credits or the journal entry is incorrect. The double-entry system is the method used in accounting. As a double-entry bookkeeping convention, all debits (always on the left) are entered before credits (always on the right). In addition to adjusting and closing entries, a *journal entry* is used to rectify errors, make reversing entries, and explain anything of an unusual nature that requires amplification.

Ledger

A *ledger* is the recipient of the information first recorded in journals. The general ledger has pages to accommodate all the accounts listed in the chart of accounts. The Accounts Receivable and Payable Ledgers have pages on which to record the details of each sale or purchase transaction. The *ledger* is a book of secondary entry.

Liabilities

Liabilities are the financial obligations of a business. Being overdrawn at the bank, large accounts payable, many loans and notes payable, and so on may be a reflection of a business in dire straits. *Liabilities* are displayed as credits on the balance sheet.

Master Column

The first column of the journals is known as the *master column*. The sum of all the columns that follow must equal the total of the master column.

Owner's Equity

It is the net worth of a business. Owner's Equity is increased each time the business activities results in a profit and as the owner makes additional investments. Conversely, owner's equity is adversely affected by losses and the owner's withdrawal of money. Owner's Equity is usually shown on the credit side of the balance sheet beneath the liabilities

Petty Cash Fund

Small amounts of cash set aside in order to reimburse individuals who have made cash purchases on behalf of the business.

Posting

The process of transferring amounts from the journals to the appropriate ledgers.

Prepaid Expense Account

The prepaid expense account keeps a record of expenses paid before they are due. It is treated as an asset (recorded on the balance sheet). With the passage of time the portion or the expense that has been consumed is transferred from the *prepaid expense account* to the profit and loss account.

Profit and Loss Items

Profit and loss items are the normal income and expense items associated with a business. At the end of the accounting period the expenses are subtracted from sales and other income items and the profit or loss is determined. This profit or loss is transferred by journal entry to the owner's equity account. The closing entry is such that all the profit and loss items become zero at the beginning of the new accounting period. As the new accounting period progresses, the new income and expense amounts build up and, at the end of the new accounting period they are, once again, transferred to owner's equity. Thus, this process is repeated each accounting period.

Purchase Journal

The purchase journal is the primary journal used to record accounts payable (liability) transactions.

Sales Journal

The sales journal is a record of the sale of goods and services rendered on credit.

Subsidiary Ledgers

A *subsidiary ledger* is a group of similar accounts whose combined balances equal the balance in a specific general ledger account. For example, Accounts Payable and Accounts Receivable are *subsidiary ledgers*. The general ledger account that summarizes a subsidiary ledger's account balances is called a "control account." The combined balance of every account in this subsidiary ledger equals the balance of accounts receivable in the general ledger. These ledgers together with the intermediate items form, what best is described as a separate set of books. They are not related to the general ledger except that the general ledger contains the totals of the amounts posted to the *subsidiary ledgers*.

Trial Balance

A trial balance is the total of all the debit and credit balances at the end of an accounting period in the general ledger. A *trial balance* also shows if the general ledger is in balance prior to making closing entries. The trial balance also serves as a worksheet for making adjusting closing entries, and provides the basis for making financial statements.

Appendix B

General Ledger Flow Chart

The following chart displays the flow of data starting from the journals (Purchase, Sales, Check Disbursements, and Cash Receipts) through the General Leger and to the Trial Balance, to form the backbone of the financial statements—the Balance Sheet and Profit and Loss Statement. See also, Appendix G.

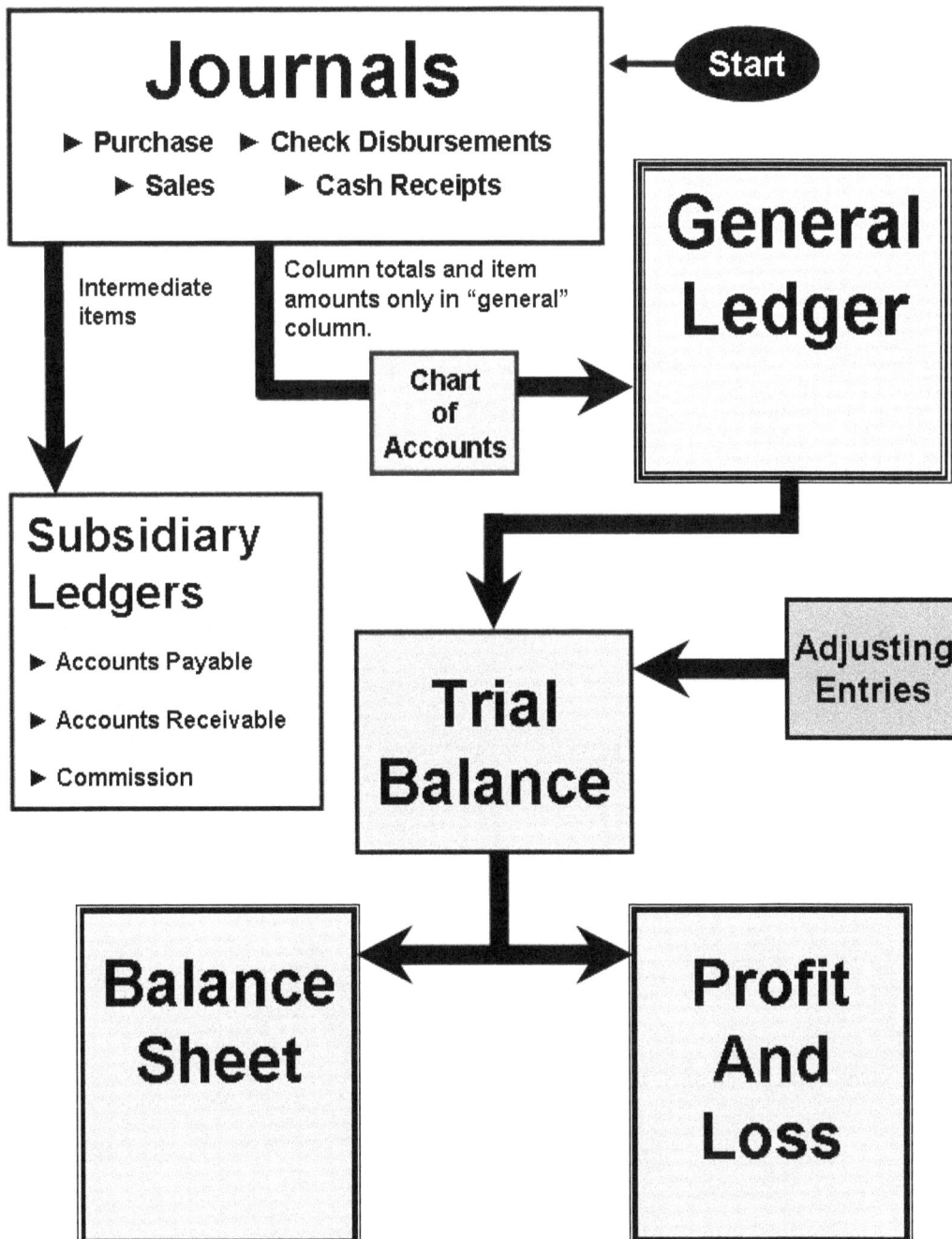

Appendix C

Purchase Journal Flow Chart

The following chart shows a Star Company purchase on credit flowing through the Purchase Journal to the General Ledger (*accounts payable control* page) and to the Accounts Receivable Subsidiary Ledger.

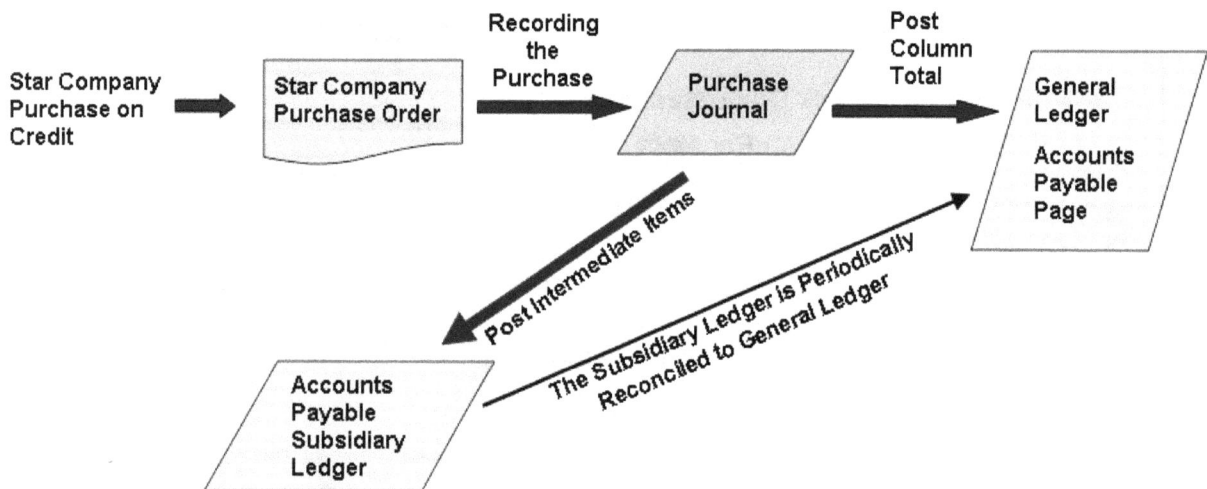

Appendix D

Sales Journal Flow Chart

The following chart shows a customer purchase on credit flowing through the Sales Journal to the General Ledger (*accounts receivable control* page) and to the Accounts Receivable Subsidiary Ledger.

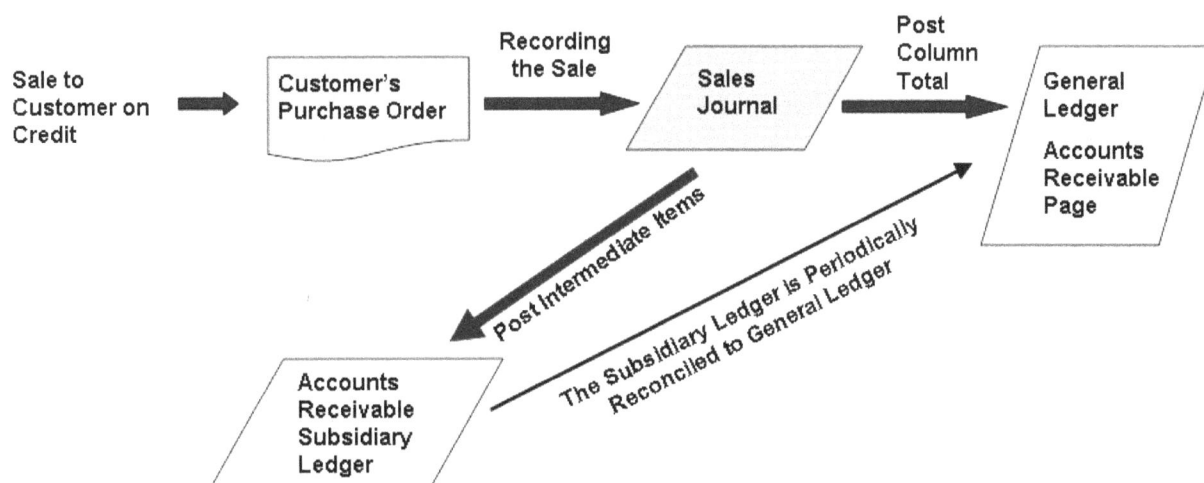

Sale to Customer on Credit → Customer's Purchase Order

Recording the Sale → Sales Journal

Post Column Total → General Ledger / Accounts Receivable Page

Post Intermediate Items → Accounts Receivable Subsidiary Ledger

The Subsidiary Ledger is Periodically Reconciled to General Ledger

Appendix E

Journal Column Flow Chart

The following chart illustrates how the totals of all the columns in the four journals—Purchase, Check Disbursement, Sales, and Cash Receipts—flow through the books of account. See Appendix G for a more detailed illustration that also shows the complete posting of the intermediate items.

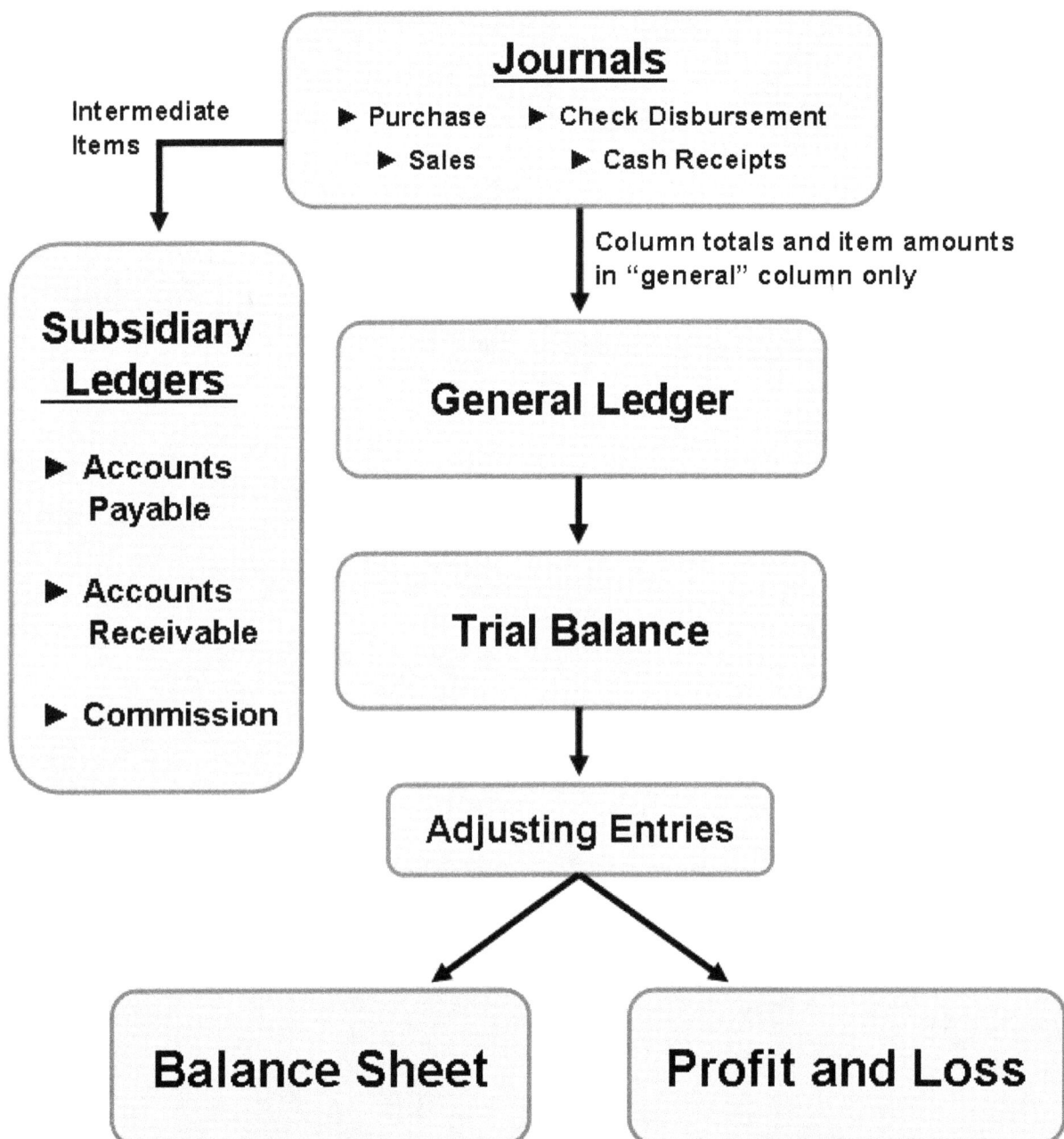

Journals
- ▶ Purchase ▶ Check Disbursement
- ▶ Sales ▶ Cash Receipts

Intermediate Items

Column totals and item amounts in "general" column only

Subsidiary Ledgers
- ▶ Accounts Payable
- ▶ Accounts Receivable
- ▶ Commission

General Ledger

Trial Balance

Adjusting Entries

Balance Sheet

Profit and Loss

Appendix F

Purchase Journal Chart

The following chart shows postings of intermediate items to subsidiary ledgers and postings of column totals to the General Ledger from the Purchase Journal.

Please note the following:

- All totals in all the journals are posted to the General Ledger.

- The intermediate items in the accounts payable column are posted to the Accounts Payable Ledger, a subsidiary ledger. Particularly observe the total of the accounts payable column has been posted to the General Ledger, but the intermediate items in the accounts payable column are posted to a subsidiary ledger, the Accounts Payable Ledger.

- All subsidiary ledgers are completely independent of the General Ledger; totals are posted to the General Ledger and intermediate items are posted to subsidiary ledgers.

- Subsidiary ledgers main purpose is to supply information to management. Since the total of the accounts payable column has already been posted to the General Ledger the information contained in subsidiary ledgers is inconsequential. Trial balances are made without referring to subsidiary ledgers.

ACCOUTS PAYABLE CONTROL GENERAL LEDGER GL 7

Date	Item	Post	Debit	Credit	Balance Debit	Balance Credit
EOM		PJ 1		3,500		

PURCHASES GENERAL LEDGER GL 52

Date	Item	Post	Debit	Credit	Balance Debit	Balance Credit
EOM		PJ 1	3,500			

Totals to General Ledger

PURCHASE JOURNAL PJ 1

Date	Account Credited	Post	Accounts Payable Credit	Purchases Debit			General	Amount Debit
EOM	Comet Co.	AP C	1,400	1,400				
EOM	Asteroid Co.	AP A	1,200	1200				
EOM	Nebula Co.	AP N	900	900				
	Total		3,500	3,500				
			GL 7	GL 52				

Intermediate Items

ACCOUNTS PAYABLE LEDGER

Name	NEBULA CO.	Terms:	2% 10 NET 30		AP N	
Date	Item	Post	Debit	Credit	Balance	
EOM		PJ 1		900		

ACCOUNTS PAYABLE LEDGER

Name:	ASTEROID CO.	Terms:	2% 10 NET 30		AP A	
Date	Item	Post	Debit	Credit	Balance	
EOM		PJ 1		1,200		

ACCOUNTS PAYABLE LEDGER

Name:	COMET CO.	Terms:	NET 30		AP C	
Date	Item	Post	Debit	Credit	Balance	
EOM		PJ 1		1,400		

Appendix G
Journal Flow Chart

The following chart details how the column totals and the intermediate item amounts in the four journals—Purchase, Check Disbursement, Sales, and Cash Receipts—flow through to the Subsidiary Ledgers and to the General Ledger.

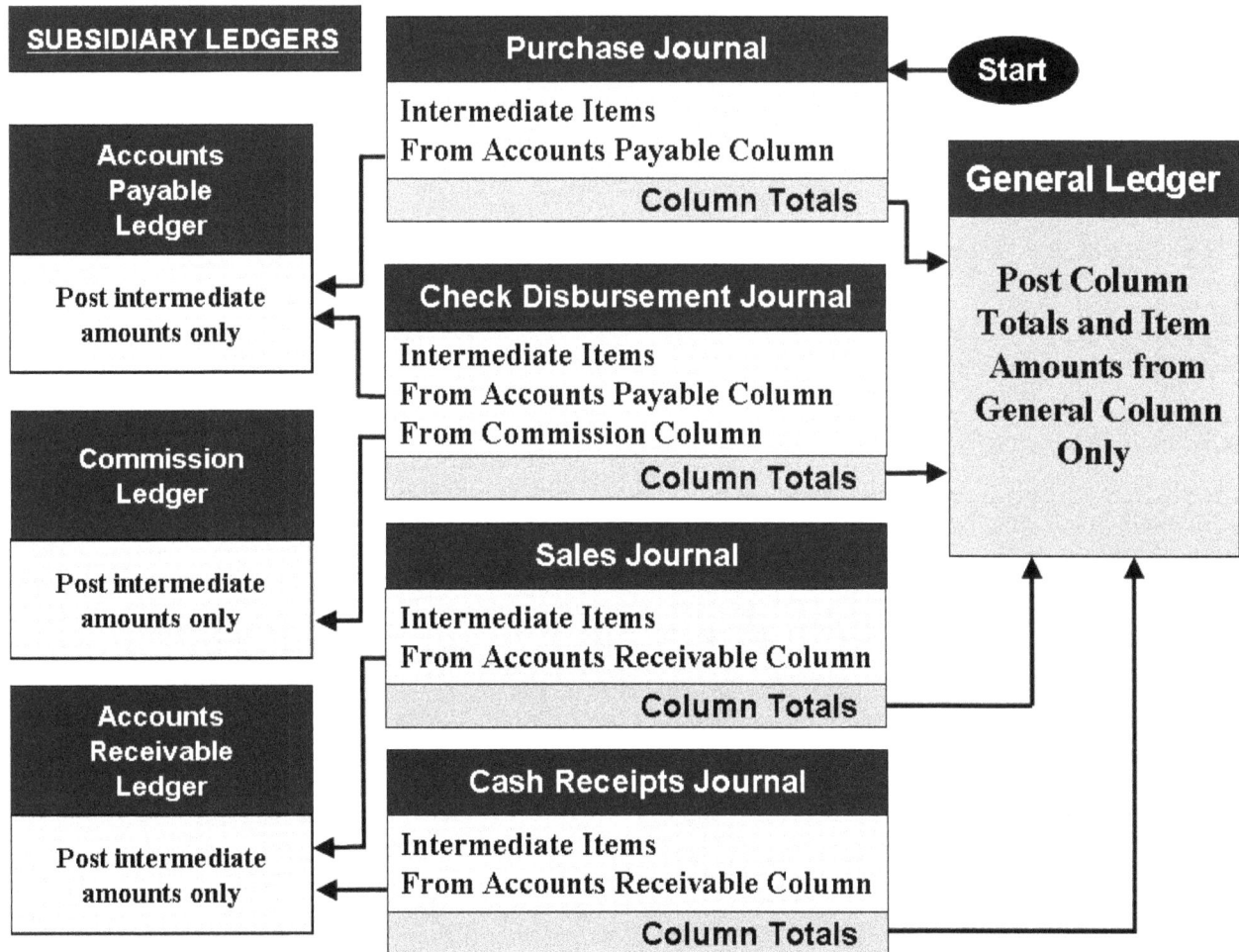

SUBSIDIARY LEDGERS

Purchase Journal

Intermediate Items
From Accounts Payable Column

Column Totals

Start

Accounts Payable Ledger

Post intermediate amounts only

General Ledger

Post Column Totals and Item Amounts from General Column Only

Check Disbursement Journal

Intermediate Items
From Accounts Payable Column
From Commission Column

Column Totals

Commission Ledger

Post intermediate amounts only

Sales Journal

Intermediate Items
From Accounts Receivable Column

Column Totals

Accounts Receivable Ledger

Post intermediate amounts only

Cash Receipts Journal

Intermediate Items
From Accounts Receivable Column

Column Totals

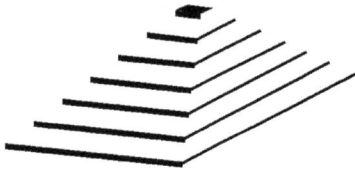

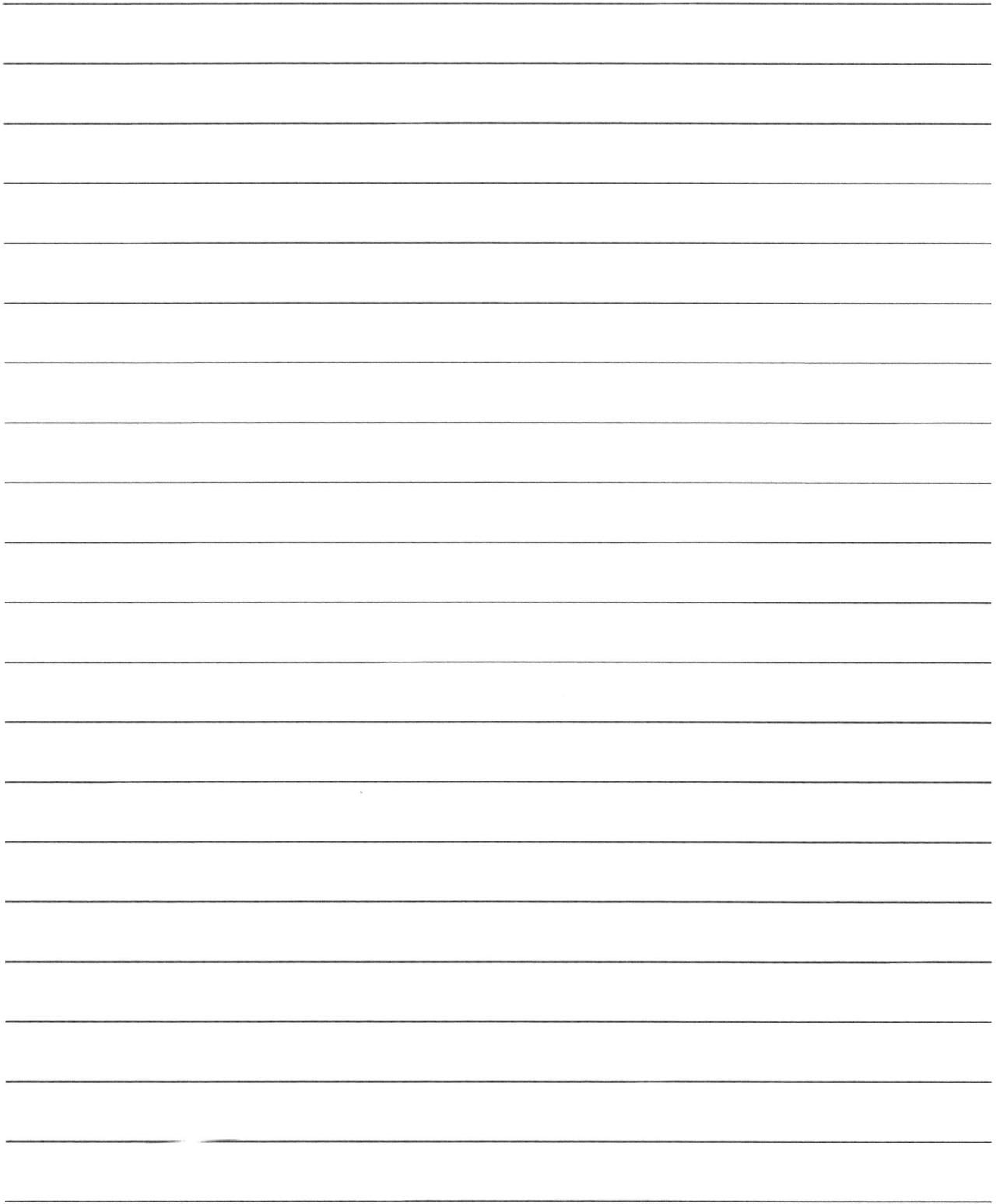

www.ingramcontent.com/pod-product-compliance
Lightning Source LLC
Chambersburg PA
CBHW062016090426
42811CB00005B/868